THE
HEROIC
PATH

The Heroic Path: Charting Your Course out of Failure and Into Purposeful Living

Copyright © 2012 David Kortje
All rights reserved.

Published by Heart & Life Publishers, Grand Rapids, Michigan.
www.heartandlife.com.

ISBN-10: 0-983992-4-4-8
ISBN-13: 978-0-983992-4-4-8

Unless otherwise noted, Scripture is taken from the HOLY BIBLE, New International Version®. Copyright ©1973, 1978, 1984 by International Bible Society. Used by permission of Zondervan.
All rights reserved.

Cover design: Brian Fowler
Interior design: Frank Gutbrod

Printed in the United States of America

Everybody wants clarity and intentionality, but few are willing to deal with hardship, struggle, and honest reflection. There is something heroic and transcendent about you—it's in your story. So much of who we are to be and what we are to bring to this world is revealed in our life experiences. We just need to know how to interpret it, and David Kortje helps us do this in *The Heroic Path*.

Gary Barkalow, Author
It's Your Call: What Are You Doing Here
Founder, The Noble Heart

Satan has convinced many Christian men that their past failures prohibit them from serving God, or even being loved by Him. David Kortje leads the attack against that lie in *The Heroic Path*. This book is a must read for any man weighed down by disappointment and in search of deliverance from the guilt produced by failure.

David Welsh, Senior Pastor
Central Christian Church, Wichita, KS

The Heroic Path is a book of tremendous insight and power—but only for those of us who have ever made mistakes! I started reading this book unaware of how much I needed to hear its message, but God used it to minister to my heart and continue the healing and restoring work that He began years ago.

Tim Spedoske, MD
Mason, Michigan

The Heroic Path is a resource that every man needs to have at the ready in his "Life Survival Kit." I very much look forward to having the opportunity to walk with groups of men through the pages of this book and through the Trail Markers that have been provided at the end of each chapter.

Rob Schmutz, Pastor
The Church at Park City

Most instruction that Christian men receive is on living a victorious life, when truth is, failure comes to us all. Little teaching is given on how to deal with that inevitable failure. *The Heroic Path* deals with all the issues: loss of self esteem, broken trust, and lasting insecurity. This book is a valuable tool for the faith.

Timothy J. King, Attorney
Speth & Kingdav

The Heroic Path by David Kortje is a must read for all men. Not only does it take a candid and honest look at the stumbling blocks most commonly encountered by men as we live our lives (and how those "things" have the power to define us), but it also reminds us that our true identity is not found in our failures but rather through the grace, love, mercy, power, and strength of God through Jesus Christ. Understanding who we are—who we really are, is essential for the road which lies ahead.

Jim Helzer, Pastor
Leon United Methodist Church

A bullseye! As men we desperately need to be reminded of the Truth of who we are, the circumstances of the battle we live in, and the MUCH greater role we were designed to play. Dr. Kortje's message is truly a much needed prescription for every man's soul.

Ryan L. Hiesterman, O.D.,
Co-founder of Wellspring Outfitters, KS

David K. Kortje

THE HEROIC PATH

*Charting Your Course out of Failure
and into Purposeful Living*

HEART & LIFE
PUBLISHERS

To Alisha, Joshua, Caleb, and Josiah.
I am painfully aware that I have failed each of you
in some very deep and personal ways.
Thank you for the forgiveness you have shown me
that has given me the courage
to walk this heroic path.

Table of Contents

Introduction *11*
Chapter 1: Our Greatest Fear *17*
Chapter 2: Ambushed *33*
Chapter 3: G1: The Girls *47*
Chapter 4: G2: The Gold *61*
Chapter 5: G3: The Glory *75*
Chapter 6: World at War *87*
Chapter 7: Jesus's Call *99*
Chapter 8: Why Me? *111*
Chapter 9: Orientation *125*
Chapter 10: For Your Eyes Only *137*
Chapter 11: Dreams, Desires, and Passion *153*
Chapter 12: Just Do It *165*
Chapter 13: Sitting at the Master's Feet *175*
Chapter 14: Bandages, Splints, and Other First Aid *187*
Chapter 15: Instrument Rating *201*
Chapter 16: Covering Your Backside *213*
Chapter 17: Weapons Training *227*
Chapter 18: Aboriginal Living Skills *245*
Chapter 19: Off with the Fig Leaf *259*
Acknowledgments *273*
David Kortje Bio *275*

Introduction

The Man on the Side of the Mountain

It was one of the strangest sights I had ever seen: a man, unshaven, sitting on a rock at 10,000 feet in Colorado in the early morning, wearing a garbage bag.

I was heading up Mount Yale with a couple of good friends. It's an imposing trek. At 14,200 feet, the round trip from the trailhead can take a good twelve hours. Most hikers, like us, begin well before sunup in order to avoid the frequent afternoon thunderstorms or evening snow. This man apparently hadn't. He told us he had started out the afternoon before, made the peak about sunset, and then gotten disoriented and lost on the way down. Weather began moving in, so he bivouacked, or set up a temporary encampment, using his trash bag as a shelter and spent the night on the mountain. He looked cold, exhausted, and dehydrated but refused any of our food, water, or assistance. Continuing on, we looked back, and our visitor was gone.

THE HEROIC PATH

We talked about that man for much of the hike. Was he a local? Perhaps a real-life mountain man? Or maybe a flatlander like us, who had narrowly escaped with his life? Perhaps he was an angel or some other majestic being sent to meet us on our journey. Whatever he was, he was definitely a metaphor: a metaphor for our lives, a metaphor for my life.

I may have planned better than he did for this peak, but if I were honest, much of the journey of my life has happened quite by surprise with equally dangerous consequences. Often I have found myself on an unknown trek, unsure of the dangers and even unaware of any risk, just meandering along, enjoying the view. That's usually when it happens.

A thundercloud forms overhead. Perhaps it's a business deal gone bad or the searing words of a loved one I've wounded. It may be the face of the man I feared I would become, staring back at me from the mirror. Or it may be some event that reminds me of dreams I will never attain. Whatever it is, instantly, like my mountain traveler, I too am forced to deal with the reality that I am somehow on a trail I can't get off and for which I am ill-prepared.

What happened? How did I get here? And why do I feel like such an idiot for not recognizing the danger earlier? A trash bag? Really? That's the best I can do? I feel like I'm an adolescent at Boy Scout camp, enduring the sneers of all of the others as my tent blows down for the third night in a row.

I doubt I'm the only one. I've spoken to many men throughout the years. I've climbed fourteeners with them, sat with them by

Introduction

campfires, enjoyed good meals with them, and met with them face-to-face during altar calls. I've heard their stories. Universally, it seems, most of us guys find ourselves at one point or another sitting in our trash bags. And we usually think it's our fault.

Regardless of who's to blame, it can be a very humbling place to be. I hate to fail. And when I do, like the man on the rock, I usually deny it, assure everyone that I'm okay and had actually planned it that way, and then try to disappear into the dawn. There's a problem, however: that damned mirror keeps reflecting back what I know of me.

But what if it's not damned? What if the mirror is in fact redeeming? Is it possible that my failings could actually teach me something about the life I was meant to live?

That is the premise of this book. Unless you have spent your entire life living in some kind of protective, aristocratic bubble, never risking anything, I think it's safe to say that at some point you, too, have failed. (And honestly, if you have lived in such a bubble, you have failed far more than you realize.) Your failure—or more likely, failures—has shaped you, for better or for worse.

Having accepted this, you have two choices. You can either go on with your life, ignoring the wound and hoping it won't come back to haunt you; or you can deal with it, learn from it, and grow from it. And that second option, my friend, is the great news I have discovered: failure not only doesn't have to define you, but it can actually serve as the catalyst that propels you to the next level of God's purpose for your life.

THE HEROIC PATH

What Is Really Going On Here?

Denial and mere existence? Or truth and growth? The choice is yours. But before you make it, you must understand something. That collapse in judgment, that misstep—it was not your fault. At least, not completely. Sure, you made the call, took the risk, drank the Kool-Aid, opened your big mouth, and so yes, in that respect you bear responsibility. But other forces were also involved: evil forces bent on your destruction. This may not be the most popular or politically correct thing to say, but I would be remiss not to tell you.

The truth of the matter is that you are in a battle. You may not recognize it, you may refuse to believe it, but that does not negate the fact. Think about it. How else can you explain the opposition you have felt for so long? I certainly believe in good old-fashioned bad luck, but when it becomes orchestrated to hit repeatedly at the heart of my dreams and desires, it is no longer just "luck."

Jesus sketches a similar portrait in John, chapter ten. Identifying us as sheep that He, the Good Shepherd, loves and longs to protect, Jesus explains that there is a reason He desires to protect us: because there is also one who is determined to destroy us. "The thief comes only to steal and kill and destroy," He states. This thief is identified in the Bible as a fallen angel named Satan, who along with his many followers has been waging war on mankind since our creation. Far from a little red man in leotards, this Satan is a master terrorist whose primary purpose is to keep you from the life that Jesus has for you.

Introduction

That's right: Jesus has a life specifically for you. "The thief comes only to steal and kill and destroy; *I have come that they may have life, and have it to the full*" (John 10:10, emphasis mine).

But before you can go on to face your failures and become all that you were meant to be, you must come to terms with this truth: You were placed here at this time in this place for a very specific purpose. Your life is not an accident, and neither are your wounds. Your life is opposed. That is why it feels like warfare out there—because it is!

If you're raising your eyebrows right about now, that's okay. I did too the first time I heard this message. But consider: If we really do have an enemy who is trying to destroy our lives, wouldn't his work would be much easier if he kept us in the dark about it? I mean, think about it. The world was abdicated to Satan in the garden, and he certainly isn't going to make his actions obvious. That doesn't mean it's not true; rather, it points to the fact that Satan is very good at camouflaging what he does.

If you already understand the stakes and the risks that are involved, then all the better, because I have some very good news to help you fight this great battle

Either way, I invite you to join me on this journey as we examine some of our personal disappointments and failings. As we do, we will build on this battle theme and on your place in God's grand story. We will take an honest look at what the Bible says on the subject.

Then we will learn how men, much like you and me, have overcome their wounds. From their examples you will discover

THE HEROIC PATH

how you too can step back into the heart of the life you were meant to live—the life you have always dreamed of living.

Of course, stepping back up to the plate only to be thrown out again is futile. The final chapters of this book will equip you with tools to help you successfully face all that the Devil, the world, or just plain life may throw at you.

I, for one, am tired of being that man on the side of the mountain in a garbage bag. I no longer want to be content with merely surviving the night; I want to flourish. I hope you feel the same way, because honestly, all of us are engaged in an epic battle, and we desperately need what *you* have to offer. You may feel as if any contribution you could make has been violated and diminished; you may have seriously questioned whether you are even qualified to fight on any longer. I know how it is because I've had those same questions. Please trust me on this: That self-doubt is not God your Father speaking. The One who created you in His image and for His purpose hasn't changed His mind about you. You are still His son created in His image, and He still has the same purpose for you as when He created you.

So come, journey with me beyond the bitter wounds of failure. Together we can discover that heroic path that you were created for.

Chapter One

Our Greatest Fear

When a man arrives at great prosperity God did it;
when he falls into disaster, he did it himself.

Benjamin Franklin

For though a righteous man falls seven times, he rises again,
but the wicked are brought down by calamity.

Proverbs 24:16

THE HEROIC PATH

As I hung up the phone, my heart sank. "How could I have missed that?" The world had come suddenly to a standstill, but my pulse was racing. Anxiety, fear, and despair circled my desk like a pride of hungry lions surrounding a wounded wildebeest as I tried desperately to reorient my thinking.

The call had been from a radiologist colleague. As a family physician, I had been treating a very sweet elderly lady for a condition that seemed rather routine. I thought she was responding, so we had continued our course of therapy over a number of months. But as time marched on, she still exhibited symptoms. Finally, I had decided to do a CAT scan to take a closer look, and that was the reason for this mid-afternoon phone call. The radiologist informed me that my patient had a number of masses inside her body, and they were spreading, the result of a malignant tumor.

She had cancer. She very likely would die.

As a young physician just a few years into my practice, I understood the role of a primary care physician. I knew the great trust that our patients put in us. Failure is not an option. Our patients come to us and pay us well to differentiate the serious from the benign, and they expect us to be right. They place their lives in our hands and are dependent on us to make the correct diagnosis—and I had not.

Calling this wonderfully sweet Christian woman into my office, I sat down and informed her of my failed diagnosis and of her very critical condition. I asked for her forgiveness and sent her on to an oncologist for further evaluation and treatment.

Our Greatest Fear

Programmed to Succeed

Few things affect a man like failure. We men are programmed to succeed. So whether it's in a business venture, a relationship, a job, as a father, or in ministry, when failure rears its ugly head, questions flood our minds. For me, the questions involved whether I should ever have been a doctor in the first place; why I always tried to take the easier, simpler route; and what my family and colleagues would think of me now, not to mention this woman who had just received the worse news of her life. At a much deeper level, my question was, "Do I really have anything to offer, or will I always be just a screw-up?"

And failure always gets the better press. Just open your newspaper or watch the evening news. Our favorite stories are of the professional athlete who got caught cheating on his wife, or the stockbroker found guilty of embezzling millions of dollars from his clients' retirement funds. Bring up a story of a man's failings and you are sure to get a lively discussion.

It doesn't have to be earth-shattering either. Recently at a religious gathering, I found myself caught up in a conversation concerning a man who had started a small Bible study only to have it fall apart. For some reason, his failure made the rest of us feel strangely better about ourselves. What's up with that?

Novels, television, and the big screen certainly don't help the matter much. Stories of our heroes typically paint the picture of a man who can do no wrong. He may be wrongly accused, but in the end he is almost always proved right. Add to that the expectations to be a perfect husband, a successful businessman, a devout churchgoer, and a self-sacrificing father, and it's no wonder that we expect perfection of ourselves and those around us.

To compound our frustration even more, we have Jesus himself telling us to "Be perfect, therefore, as your heavenly Father is perfect" (Matthew 5:48).

As we real-world men watch, listen to, and read all these standards for manly perfection, one thing becomes glaringly obvious: that ain't us. Something must be wrong with us. Evidently we really are screw-ups with nothing to offer. That conclusion can lead us to true failure. As the Chinese proverb states, "Failure is not falling down, but refusing to get up."

Since men can't live for long in a world of failure, we begin searching for other areas where we can succeed. My study at home, my "man-cave," is lined with over fifty trophies and plaques that I have won through the years racing motocross and Jet Skis. Mind you, most of these were not real wins. In fact, I have only one first-place trophy. Most of the others came from competing against other "old guys" like me (sometimes just a handful), during which time, by luck or fate or maybe just the planets aligning properly, I managed to cross the finish line ahead of the rest. In the grand scheme of motocross, I am a mediocre rider, but still the trophies do something for me. They stroke a part of my ego that feels inadequate.

Most men have a "trophy room." It may be their list of all of the corporate deals they've made, the girls they've had, or the awards they've received. Maybe it is a garage full of toys or a photo album filled with pictures. It may even be altruistic: ministries they have supported, Sunday school classes they've taught, or even children they have raised. Many of these trophies are good things in themselves. Good or bad, however, they arise from a common need. Men require successes they can point to because in the deepest part of their heart they are looking for something. They are looking for significance.

And almost universally, if you ask a man—and if he is brave enough to be honest with you—he will admit that he hasn't found that significance. At least, not completely. A surprising number of men will tell you that they have failed far more often than they have succeeded. And it is this sense of failure that largely directs a man's life.

Since it is significance that we seek, and since failure prevents that significance, most of us will find ourselves adjusting our lives to ensure our success—and hence, our significance. Moreover, we will avoid at all costs the people, places, or things that we have not done well with.

Tucking Tail

Choosing your battles isn't always a bad thing. At just under five feet, ten inches tall, with a vertical leap of about six inches, I have never excelled at basketball. I tried it a few times in middle school and in the driveway, but I quickly surmised that it was not my sport, so I don't play basketball. I don't think that is a critical mistake; in fact, you could make an excellent argument that I would be wasting valuable time if I spent every waking hour out on the hardwood working on my lay-ups. Some failures point us away from things we were never designed to do.

We must be careful, though. Basketball and your place in God's grand adventure are not the same thing (unless, of course, your name is Michael Jordan). I have spoken to many men who concluded, after years of arguments and disappointments, that they were not cut out for marriage (at least, not the one they were in at the time). If you have experienced the pain of a divorce, I recognize that every situation is unique, and some marriages are not salvageable. I am not trying to point a finger at anyone, particularly since my own marriage has been on the precipice of divorce more than once. That said, there is a vast difference between walking away from a God-ordained institution and walking away from a weekend pastime. The former is by far the one that wounds the deepest.

The truth is, we have all tucked tail and run at various times in our lives, and those times have affected us in profound ways. I once knew a brilliant businessman who had provided quite nicely for his family. He and his wife had a beautiful home, traveled to exquisite places, and sent their children to the finest schools. The man was also more than generous with both his finances and his time, offering them sacrificially in a multitude of ways.

Then it all fell apart. Job losses, poor choices, and just plain bad luck eroded the man's fortunes until, broke and feeling the full weight of his failure, he found himself alone on the roadside with a revolver in his hand, pointed at his head.

This man would tell you that he was rescued by God. But many aren't so fortunate, or they are so enveloped by their pain that they can't see God. Despair devastates the lives of far too many men before cancer and heart disease ever get a chance to destroy their bodies.

What is it about failure that has such a powerful effect on us? Why is it that a moment of indiscretion or an unsuccessful ministry—or a missed field goal, for that matter—can take us out, sometimes forever? What is it about these wounds that seem so defining?

Falling or taking a hit is one thing, but it's really what follows that is so destructive. We begin to make vows: "I will never try that again," or, "I must not be called to this," or, "I am disqualified; God could never use me now."

Joseph

The Bible is so filled with stories of failures that one begins to wonder whether failure isn't a prerequisite for being used by God. Joseph is a prime example. The second youngest in a family of twelve brothers, he begins early in his life to sense that there is something unique about him and his place in God's story.

Joseph has a couple of dreams, and in them he sees images, first of twelve sheaves of grain and next of the sun, the moon, and eleven stars, all honoring him (Genesis 37:5–10). He interprets these dreams—correctly, I might add—as his brothers bowing down to him. Unfortunately, in his youth and immaturity, he makes the mistake of telling his family about the dreams (most likely with an air of "see what God told me"). His brothers, as brothers can be, dismiss him as a fool. To make matters worse, his father has a special jacket hand made for him (the coat of many colors) as a personal gift to his favorite son. Instead of receiving it humbly, Joseph shows it off to his brothers, wearing it everywhere and letting the whole family know that there is something extraordinary about him. It backfires. Instead, the brothers plot to kill him, but at the last minute they change their minds and choose instead to sell him as a slave to passing merchants on their way to Egypt.

Once in Egypt, he is purchased by a good man, Potiphar. Joseph, now with some of the maturity that comes with years and hard knocks, works hard for his new master, and soon he is put in charge of Potiphar's entire household.

You know the rest of the story: Potiphar (likely a workaholic) is never home, and his wife gets lonely. When our hero refuses her advances, she accuses him of trying to rape her. Joseph finds himself locked in a cold prison cell, and this time it's not his fault. He was trying to do the right thing, but the result is still the same.

If I were Joseph, right about now I'd be thinking that maybe there really is nothing to my life. I can understand God's discipline for the arrogance of my youth, but how do I make sense of these latest events?

Most of us would likely die in that prison. Not Joseph. He continues to pursue the life that is ahead of him. Again he finds himself in a position of leadership, albeit as a prisoner, and eventually he interprets two more dreams—other men's dreams instead of his own this time. And what do you know! Three years later (no one ever said things happen rapidly in God's perfect timing), the pharaoh is told of Joseph's gift, and this small-town boy goes from leading the laundry crew to leading a nation.

Not until years later do we begin to understand what motivates Joseph. He has brought his entire family to Egypt to save them from a great famine. Eventually Joseph's father, Jacob, dies. Joseph's brothers fear that their younger brother—who now has absolute power and before whom they are indeed kneeling as Joseph's dreams had foretold—may finally take vengeance on them for that whole slave-trading thing of years gone by.

"But Joseph said to them, 'Don't be afraid. Am I in the place of God? You intended to harm me, but God intended it for good to accomplish what is now being done, the saving of many lives'" (Genesis 50:19–20).

Fear or Sonship

Paul says it this way: "I consider that our present sufferings are not worth comparing with the glory that will be revealed in us. The creation waits in eager expectation for the sons of God to be revealed … And we know that in all things God works for the good of those who love him, who have been called according to his purpose" (Romans 8:18–19, 28).

That's *you* whom Paul is speaking to: those "sons of God" that the entire creation is waiting for. Just a few verses earlier he establishes that "those who are led by the Spirit of God are sons of God. For you did not receive a spirit that makes you a slave again to fear, but you received the Spirit of sonship" (vv. 14–15).

That is our crux, isn't it: the spirit of fear. We fear there is no significance to our lives, no greater plan. We miss the big picture. As men, we tend to interpret our lives in the context of the moment, and it is in that moment when the floor has fallen out from under us—when the bill collectors are knocking, the attorney is calling, the chaos is raging—that the spirit of fear can engulf us like a tsunami, threatening to destroy all that we have built.

But "you did not receive a spirit that makes you a slave again to fear … you received a Spirit of sonship." How we need to allow that truth to root itself firmly into our hearts! We have been changed, miraculously and permanently transformed. This is more than a mere feel-good, positive mental image; it is a powerful truth of our faith.

Understanding your position as a son of our King changes everything. The battle becomes a training ground, the fear becomes a lie from our enemy, and the failures become gifts. That's right, *gifts*. The American author Napoleon Hill said that "failure is nature's plan to prepare you for greatness." I would modify that a bit and say it is God's plan to prepare you for the greatness He has intended for you all along. Not that God has caused all of your failures or indiscretions; rather, He is waiting to use them to bring you into the fullness of the life He has always planned for you.

The apostle Paul's life offers a fascinating case study on how God uses failure. Paul's birth name was Saul, and Saul was one of those men who had likely plotted out the course of his life from a young age. Born of Hebrew parents, he was as devout in his faith as any man of his time—in his own words, a "Hebrew of Hebrews." He was also a Roman citizen, a status that afforded him opportunities and privileges unavailable to non-citizens.

Furthermore, Saul was educated by the great rabbi Gamaliel. Not your everyday Sunday school teacher, this guy was kind of the Rick Warren or James Dobson of his day, highly respected and a man of considerable influence. Saul took full advantage of his heritage and his training. His heart was to follow God to the far reaches of the universe. But he made one critical mistake: he missed the Promised One. Jesus was walking the earth, literally, while Saul was being trained, and Saul missed Him. In fact, he didn't just miss Jesus; he decided that Jesus was the enemy.

Most scholars believe that Saul's conversion experience on the road to Damascus occurred within a year of the crucifixion, which makes it very possible that Saul was present during the trial and execution of the Son of God. You just can't let Jesus down much more than that.

Talk about failure! And it gets even worse. Saul headed off on a mission to hunt down and kill or imprison those who were following Jesus. No wonder the disciple Ananias argued when the Lord asked him to find Saul and restore his sight.

"'Lord,' Ananias answered, 'I have heard many reports about this man and the harm he has done to the saints in Jerusalem'" (Acts 9:13).

But you see, Saul's failure was really a gift. What a testimony! A highly educated, devoutly religious Jew became a follower of Jesus. Paul—the new name he received with his new life—took full advantage of his miraculous story, using it on numerous occasions as he proclaimed how Jesus had changed his life.

What if he had not? What if Paul had embraced his failure and chosen to live with the guilt and embarrassment of it all? How did he move on? The answer, I believe, lies in Paul's understanding of what Jesus accomplished in him.

Teleios

To the church in Corinth, Paul wrote: "Therefore, if anyone is in Christ, he is a new creation; the old has gone, the new has come!" (2 Corinthians 5:17). And to the Philippian church he boldly stated, "But one thing I do: Forgetting what is behind and straining toward what is ahead, I press on toward the goal to win the prize for which God has called me heavenward in Christ Jesus" (Philippians 3:13–14). Paul understood that something in him had changed when he accepted the sacrifice of Jesus as his own. He understood that he was no longer the man he had been.

Sure, he had failed, and sure, he struggled with his failure. But in Christ he was now a new creation, and as a new creation he identified himself by what Jesus knew of him, not what his past "proved" of him.

As men, we have all experienced similar failures and found ourselves outside of God's plan for our lives. For some of us, our failures are glaringly obvious and painful. You may be facing, or have experienced, jail time, foreclosure, or a divorce. Maybe you have been caught red-handed at something that has left your reputation forever marred.

Or you may just sense that something is missing in your walk with Christ. You began your life of faith with passion, but somehow the years and the busy-ness of life have left you just trying to hang on. Christianity has become less of a relationship and more of a ritual.

Perhaps you have found a way to move on from your failings, but still the battles rage and the drive for perfection continues to haunt you.

Which brings us back to the words of Jesus: "Be perfect, therefore, as your heavenly Father is perfect" (Matthew 5:48). The Greek word used here for *perfect* is *teleios* (pronounced tel'-i-os). It implies completeness, as in maturity. Some have suggested that Jesus was simply trying to point out the obvious here, that apart from Him we have no hope of hitting the standard, which is a perfectly sinless life. That interpretation has some truth to it; certainly it is only in Christ that we are changed and made perfect. But I also believe that Jesus was pointing us *to* something—toward a realistic goal He intends us to reach for.

Jesus's brother James wrote years later that we should consider it joy whenever we face trials, "because [we] know that the testing of [our] faith develops perseverance. Perseverance must finish its work so that [we] may be mature and complete, not lacking anything" (James 1:2–4). The word translated as "complete" is that same Greek word, *teleios*. The implication is not that we will never fail—otherwise, all of the great heroes of our faith would be disqualified. No, the implication is that we *will* fail, that we *will* be wounded (what else would you expect in a war?), but that our very failings become opportunities for us to mature (*teleios*) in our understanding of what Christ has accomplished in us.

I love this quote by a gentleman named Walter Brunell: "Failure is the tuition that we pay for success." That's true not only in business and personal endeavors; it is also true of our spiritual lives. Our enemy wants to convince us that failure disqualifies us, but our King desires to use our failures to train us. For how long? Until we are complete, not lacking anything. In other words, for the rest of our lives.

If we have any hope of walking this life in Christ, this grand adventure that He has invited us to, we must learn not only to survive our missed diagnoses, our growing apathy, our defunct businesses and relationships, but also to embrace them as opportunities to be trained and fathered by our King. It is only by doing so that we can change our failures from death blows to stepping stones toward a greatness we would never know if we had never failed. Unfortunately, we can't plan for failure. It almost always comes unannounced. Seldom are we prepared, and so we must be ready to act in an instant. We must develop a mindset to survive the ambush.

TRAIL MARKERS

1. What were your emotions and thoughts in the wake of a personal failure?
2. Does hearing of another man's failings sometimes make you feel better about yourself? Why do you think this is?
3. What does your "trophy room" look like? How much would you say you value your trophies?
4. What vows have you made in response to a failure?
5. Read Romans 8:15 again. Do you believe that this verse applies to you?
6. In your own words, define *teleios*. In what parts of your life might God currently be developing teleios in you? How might those areas be gifts?

Chapter Two

Ambushed

*Am'bush, n. [**am**-boosh]:*
An act or instance of attacking unexpectedly
from a concealed position.

Dictionary.com

Dear friends, do not be surprised at the painful trial you are suffering, as though something strange were happening to you.

1 Peter 4:12

THE HEROIC PATH

Journalist Tom Brokaw referred to them as "the Greatest Generation": the men and women coming out of the Great Depression and living through the perilous times of World War II. I recently read the story of one such man.

Stan Angleton was a waist gunner on a B-24 bomber flying with the 376th HBG (Heavy Bombardment Group). Like so many other men of his day, he had been drafted into the Army Air Corps and then sent off to fight in a distant land an ocean away from the life he had known. I doubt it was what Stan had envisioned for his life when he was a young boy growing up on the Kansas prairie, but still he went. It was what he was called to do. It was what all men his age were being called to do.

Stan performed his job with passion and with honor, flying fifteen missions out of Italy. The sixteenth mission started like so many others. The morning was overcast and the air cool. Three days earlier, his crew had celebrated Christmas with another successful mission. Today they were to rendezvous with support from a fighter squadron and then proceed to bomb a German-run ball bearing base in northern Italy.

Unfortunately, the group missed their rendezvous point with the fighters; yet instead of turning around, these brave men decided to go on with their assignment. Flying north across the Adriatic Sea, the seventeen planes of the 376th Heavy Bombardment Group suddenly found themselves surrounded by seventy-five to one hundred German Luftwaffe fighters. The larger, slower bombers were sitting ducks, and the German fighters began picking them off one by one. Planes exploded as burning fuel began to detonate the bombs on board. Most men never had a chance. Stan Angleton was one of the "lucky ones" (his words). After helping a few of his injured crewmen don parachutes, he jumped with them before their plane went down. Yet despite his heroic efforts, Angleton could do nothing but watch as two of his fellow crewmen died before even making it to the ground.

Stan's personal escape from the guns of the Luftwaffe didn't end in safety. He was captured in German-occupied territory and shipped to a POW camp.

I cannot begin to fathom what that day must have been like for this young, twenty-year-old man from Kansas. Serving his president and his country as best and as honorably as he could, he hadn't asked for any of this. He knew that he was fighting a great evil. He knew the risks and all that was at stake. Still, he must have wondered, *Why?* Why him? Why now? Why didn't his group turn around? Why couldn't he have been born ten years later? And what was going to happen now? Kansas had never seemed so far away.

We Aren't in Kansas Anymore

I have never been in a physical war. I have never been shot down by enemy aircraft and have never spent even a day in a POW camp. Yet I too have been ambushed, and I suspect that you have as well.

Your ambush may have been abrupt and deliberate, perhaps a betrayal or a personal attack. Maybe it was a coworker or ministry

THE HEROIC PATH

leader who suddenly turned on you or a rival who carefully planned the whole incident.

Or the ambush may have been one of your own doing. Failing to heed the warnings or trying to manipulate your situation, you found yourself suddenly caught in a crossfire that left no escape. You may have seen it coming, or you may have been caught totally off guard.

Then again, perhaps your experience was more of a slow, steady fall. You felt sure that eventually things would turn around, that sooner or later you would find a way out. But your plane kept arcing relentlessly earthward, your efforts to save yourself proved futile, and ultimately you found yourself plummeting toward the ground. Now, dazed and disoriented, you keep replaying the same old scene in your mind, trying to figure out what went wrong.

Whatever your downfall was like, you and all of us have one thing in common with Stan Angleton: we are now in a place where we never dreamed of finding ourselves, and we wonder why. Even more importantly, we wonder if anything can possibly save us. Do we even want to be saved? I mean, what do we have left to offer?

So far from where we started, so many injuries, so many fears. Is there really any reason to try again?

That is just where our enemy wants us.

The Battle Set against Us

The battle that has been set against your life, against the life that God would have for you, is every bit as deliberate and calculated as the battle that sent Stan Angleton parachuting out of his broken

Ambushed

B-24 bomber on that cold December day in 1942. You have likely been led to believe otherwise. You have been told that it was just bad luck, or bad choices, or fate. You may even be convinced that it was really what you wanted or perhaps even a sign from God that you were never meant to fight in this war. All of these notions may have a hint of truth in them, perhaps just enough to convince you to stop looking for any other answers. Yet other answers are just what you need because it is only in discovering the truth of your life that you can recover your bearings and discover the path back to real life.

And you can find that path. The Bible is filled with stories of men who were taken out, shot down, by an enemy with inconceivable skill, only to rediscover the life that God had for them. Adam mistakenly chose the "greater" knowledge of good and evil. Moses tried his own hand at rescuing his people. David took a break from the battle and sought comfort in the arms of another man's wife. Elijah served God faithfully only to find himself depressed and suicidal, asking God to take his life.

The New Testament is likewise filled with ambush victims. Peter, arrogant and proud, failed his King at our Lord's time of greatest need. The thief on the cross beside Jesus completely missed his place in the story until his final hours of life. And Saul of Tarsus, who had committed himself wholly to following God, suddenly realized that he had spent the first half of his life on the wrong page altogether.

Yet each of these men discovered something deeper, something truer about the time he was caught up in. Each discovered that it wasn't his failure that defined him. Rather, it was the grace of God that restored him back into the battle and reminded him who he truly was.

In Hiding

One of my favorite Bible characters is a man named Gideon. We first meet this son of Joash the Abiezrite in the book of Judges, chapter six. It seems that Gideon's people, the Israelites—the nation that had been uniquely set apart for God and had received direct revelation from God regarding what their lives should be like—had once again done evil in the eyes of the Lord (Judges 6:1). In consequence, for the last seven years Israel had come under the oppressive and unrelenting tyranny of the Midianites, a people so vast in number that it was impossible to count them. Week after week, month after month, and year after year, this enemy had been striking terror into the hearts of the Israelites.

Gideon himself had by no means risen to the occasion. In Judges 6:11, we find him hiding … in a wine press. Not making wine, mind you; wine was for a time of peace and celebration. No, Gideon was threshing wheat—making bread, just trying to survive and hoping that no one would notice him. He was doing okay by himself. He had stayed alive for the last seven years and made the best out of a difficult situation. But he was not living out the life God had planned for him when all of his days "were written in [the heavenly] book before one of them came to be" (Psalm 139:16).

Fortunately, for "God's gifts and his call are irrevocable" (Romans 11:29). Gideon may have forgotten, but God hadn't. So "the angel of the Lord appeared to Gideon, [and] he said, 'The Lord is with you, mighty warrior'" (Judges 6:12).

That greeting just cracks me up. Was God making fun of Gideon? Was he being sarcastic and just pointing out the obvious, that this man hiding in an eight-foot hole was anything but a mighty warrior?

No, God knew something about Gideon, something that had been true all along but had been lost in the repercussions of war. God knew that Gideon was called to greatness.

Gideon knew it too, or had known it. But he had a question—a very, very good question. Perhaps *the* question that we have all asked, "If the Lord is with us, why has all this happened to us? Where are all His wonders that our fathers told us about?" (Judges 6:13). Obviously life circumstances had not worked out as Gideon had planned. Whatever he once had been, he no longer was, and his understandable deduction was that God must not have any particular purpose for him.

An Evil Truth

That is such a dangerous conclusion to make. Countless men have missed the call of God on their lives by buying into our friend Gideon's way of thinking. Seriously, haven't you sometimes asked the same questions as Gideon? I know I have. The truth of our Christian faith demands that we pose that inquiry, for we profess a God who is all-powerful, all-knowing, and always present, a God who is intimately linked to every aspect of our lives. If there was a place that He had for us, some master-plan, then surely He would have arranged for it to happen. Clearly all of this—whatever "this" is—would never have happened to us ... unless God isn't really for us.

But what if there were another explanation—one that we missed, that we had somehow failed to consider. What if the Bible really is true and God does love us? What if He truly does have great plans for our lives, "plans to prosper [us] and not to harm [us]; plans to give [us] a hope and a future" (Jeremiah 29:11)? Could there be another explanation for where we are right now?

An enemy opposing us could explain such a dilemma. What if it's true? What if we have such an enemy, one who has intercepted communications and realized the place our King has for us in this great battle? What if he fears us walking in that call of God? Surely this enemy would do whatever was in his power to sabotage our threat to his agenda. Nothing would be off-limits. As the saying goes, "All's fair in love and war."

I wrote my first book, *The Unseen War*, specifically to expose this spiritual battle.[1] The book describes our enemy: not the Luftwaffe but Satan, the same being who was evicted from the throne room of God and now roams the earth "like a roaring lion looking for someone to devour" (1 Peter 5:8). Satan is called the Deceiver and a liar, and he has done well in living up to his reputation. Your life, like Gideon's, will only make sense as you

---

[1] David Kortje, *The Unseen War: Winning the Fight for Life* (Mobile, Alabama: Parson Place Press, 2009)

begin to understand that this enemy seeks to undermine the unique mission that your King, Jesus, has sent you to fulfill.

The underlying theme of warfare explains God's response to Gideon's questions. "The Lord turned to him and said, 'Go in the strength you have and save Israel out of Midian's hand. Am I not sending you?'" (Judges 6:14). It's interesting that God didn't really answer our young warrior's questions. To God the answer was obvious. Of course your life has been opposed, Gideon. Of course things haven't worked out as planned. You are in a war, Gideon! Bombs are dropping, bullets are flying, and you have been hit. But you are still breathing, aren't you? Go in the strength that you have—or did you forget: I am sending you.

Strength in Weakness

Many of us struggle like Gideon. We may believe that God sent us to fulfill His purposes once upon a time, or we may have wished to believe it. But now … so much has happened. The optimism of youth has given way to the realism of life. "Been there, done that," has become our favorite T-shirt. Adjustments have been made, game plans changed, and now we seriously doubt that God ever sent us at all.

But God doesn't change His mind like the shifting sand. You may have forgotten, but He hasn't. Either He created you with purpose or He didn't create you at all.

Moses discovered this truth. He knew that he had been set apart for greatness, and so at the age of forty, he decided it was time to do something about it. Seeing an Egyptian beating a fellow

THE HEROIC PATH

Israelite, he stepped in and killed the Egyptian. Unfortunately, no one seemed to appreciate his heroics, and he soon found himself running for his life.

Moses spent the next forty years in despair and failure, his life reduced from royalty to that of a shepherd tending sheep. Like so many of us, Moses just continued on, forgetting, as much as he could, his failed past.

But as with Gideon, God's call on Moses's life had not changed. When Moses was eighty years old (read that eight-zero), God appeared to him and reminded him again who he was. "I am sending you to Pharaoh to bring my people the Israelites out of Egypt" (Exodus 3:10–11). Moses's response was not unlike ours: "Who am I, that I should go to Pharaoh and bring the Israelites out of Egypt?" He had forgotten also.

God's words to Moses were essentially the same as His words to Gideon—and to us: "Go in the strength that you have, for I will be with you." You see, it's really not about our strength. In fact, God loves it when we feel as if we have no strength left at all; that is when God's strength shines. It is when men are in a position of humble dependence on His power that God uses them most effectively, whether it is David as a young boy killing the giant with a single stone, or Samson as a blind fool avenging God's people, or Saul as a misdirected zealot, bringing life to a people who had never known God. Our God delights in raising men from the ashes of their own failings.

Have you felt the pain of your failures? Have you suddenly found yourself in unfamiliar territory, wounded, limping, shell-shocked, and wondering how you got there? Have you forgotten what it was that God had for you, or maybe just decided that you were not the man for that job, that battle? Has the enemy ambushed you and left you wishing that you had never left Kansas in the first place? If so, then this book is for you. You see, I too have been there, and I have discovered a powerful truth: It is not my wound that defines me, but rather what I allow God to do with that wound.

Allow me to tell you the rest of Stan Angleton's story. He was captured and sent to a German POW camp, Stalag 17B. Five thousand American prisoners were being held there toward the end of World War II along with many other Allied prisoners. In the cold and snow of winter, without heat or hot water, the men survived on rutabaga soup and potatoes.

Fifteen months after Angleton's capture, the end of the war was quickly approaching and the Germans knew they needed to evacuate the prisoners. Stan Angleton understood that this very likely meant he would be killed, so he planned his escape. With the crafting and cunning of 007, he succeeded. For two weeks, he made his way back through enemy territory until he was picked up by American forces advancing on Europe.

I spoke with Stan Angleton a few days ago. He is eighty-seven years old, still married to his wife of sixty-four years, and enjoying life. As he speaks, you can detect a richness and depth in his voice that you only hear in those who have been through great battles.

I believe God is once again raising up a Greatest Generation of men. I believe we are to be that generation, heroes of our own battlefields. And I believe we can be—because, like all of God's great men of the past, many of us have felt the sting of failure and the pain of our own vain efforts. We have struggled firsthand with our weakness, yet we have also been called to much more. We have been invited on a journey, a journey down a heroic path.

Much is a stake, and it will take all that we are as men to move forward. Before we do though, we must visit the past and examine the wounds that we have received. Many of those wounds are self-inflicted. Others have been the result of life's circumstances. Most are felt as failures that have resulted as we have pursued one or more of what I will introduce in the next chapter as the "Three Gs."

Examining one's own missteps can be humbling for sure, even painful. It requires courage and an unrelenting willingness to expose the darkness that held us captive. But it is the only way to recover from the ambush and begin charting a course to freedom.

TRAIL MARKERS

1. Try to put yourself in Stan Angleton's shoes. How would you feel if, having done what you were supposed to, you found yourself in a POW camp?
2. Have you ever been ambushed? What happened? How did it feel?
3. Read the story of Gideon in Judges 6:1–23. What part of the account stands out to you? Why?
4. Have you ever asked the same question as Gideon in verse 13: "If God is for us, why has all of this happened?" Have you ever doubted that God had a specific plan for you?
5. How has the passage of years affected you? Do you sometimes feel as if, like Moses, you have tried and failed, and now you are reduced to tending sheep? Have you lost some of the passion of your youth?
6. How do you view men like Stan Angleton who have been through the terrors of war and somehow not only survived but thrived?

Chapter Three

G1: The Girls

Beauty is unbearable, drives us to despair, offering us for a minute the glimpse of an eternity that we should like to stretch out over the whole of time.

Albert Camus

Then the Lord God made a woman from the rib he had taken out of the man, and he brought her to the man. The man said, "This is now bone of my bones and flesh of my flesh; she shall be called 'woman,' for she was taken out of man."

Genesis 2:22–23

THE HEROIC PATH

My statistics professor in college constantly reminded my class that "figures don't lie, but liars can figure." His point, of course, was that you can manipulate statistics to say whatever you want them to say.

Be that as it may, there are some pretty sobering numbers out there about men and what Christianity calls sexual sin. A quick Google search turns up multiple sites stating that anywhere from thirty-seven to sixty percent of men will have an extramarital affair at some point in their lives. And much higher numbers of men admit to a habit of pornography. At one of the popular Promise Keepers events in 1996, half of the men who attended admitted to viewing pornography within the week leading to the event. Perhaps even more sobering is that while fifty-seven percent of pastors say addiction to pornography is the most sexually damaging issue they deal with in their congregations, a *Christianity Today* survey in 2000 found that thirty-three percent of clergy admitted to visiting sexually explicit websites.[2]

My own pseudo-research has found very similar results. As I have talked with counselors, pastors, and men's leaders about the primary issues that they see taking men out of the battle, their first response has almost universally involved some form of sexual temptation.

The apostle John described what the world has to offer outside of Jesus: "the lust of the flesh and the lust of the eyes and the boastful pride of life" (1 John 2:16, NASB). A friend of mine used to call these the "Three Gs": the Girls, the Gold, and the Glory.

---

[2] Figures obtained from the Ethics & Religious Liberty Commission website: http://erlc.com/issues/quick-facts/por/.

He said it was either one of these three or some combination thereof that the enemy would use to vie for the hearts of men.

And isn't that what we see every time we turn on the television? The commercials promise us that if we buy this product or drink that beverage, the ladies will swarm to us, or our bank accounts will swell, or those around us will recognize that we have finally arrived. Then if we switch over to the news, well, oh my! There's the latest dirt on one more guy who has chosen to pursue one of the Three Gs to the point of destroying his life, his career, or his reputation.

So it behooves us to take a hard look at these Three Gs. Let's start with the Girls. Nothing in all of creation captures a man's emotions and imagination like a woman. Created in the image of God, she is a portrait of His beauty, His compassion, and His invitation to intimacy. And can we just say from the beginning that this is a good thing! God intended women to be alluring, to arouse a man's desire for intimacy—for God himself is alluring. Being a woman is in itself a God-like quality. Isn't that what we say of the most physically beautiful women: that they are goddesses?

Unfortunately, it is these same God-like qualities of women that make them such dangerous territory. The billboards, the magazine covers, Hollywood ... all of them scream, "Come, experience ecstasy and freedom from the craziness of life with her." In other words, come and experience God.

And we buy it. I did. As I shared in my first book, *The Unseen War*,[3] my life and my marriage were almost shattered by an

---

[3] David Kortje, *The Unseen War: Winning the Fight for Life* (Mobile, Alabama: Parson Place Press, 2009)

extramarital affair. Allow me to rephrase that: my life and marriage *were* shattered. It was the most toxic, lethal poison that I have ever experienced, and it is nothing short of a miracle that I am here today, still married, writing to you about that time.

Mob Riot

What surprised me most about the affair was that it was not the sex that drew me, nor was it the sex that caused the most fallout. Don't get me wrong, I knew exactly what I was getting into, and if I had broken things off before the woman and I became intimate, then the collateral damage would have been much less. But it was what Satan did after the affair that created the greatest chaos.

You see, by opening that door, I invited an army of enemy forces into the very heart of my camp. I felt literally surrounded, with swords slicing and bullets flying from every direction. It was no longer just lust that I was fighting. Now it was accusations and embarrassment. It was the reality of my failure as a husband, the realization of how deeply I had betrayed my wife. It was what my infidelity meant to her and how she interpreted my feelings toward her. It was the recognition of what a hypocrite I had been and a real sense of how deeply disappointed and disgusted God must be with me. And no matter what I did, whether pray, apologize, repent, or redirect, another barrage of arrows awaited me at every turn.

When you're in the thick of such circumstances, you feel like you can no longer breathe, as if your next minute on the battlefield will be your last. You feel an overwhelming urge to run. It may be back to the arms of your lover. It may be just *away*—away from everything: end your marriage, quit the ministry, resign your position, maybe even end your life. If "hope deferred makes the heart sick," then hope lost is surely the death of the heart.

This is where the hardest part of the battle lies. Our enemy is an accomplished warrior, and he understands how important it is to finish off his opponents. We've all seen the movies when this didn't happen: a character gets shot, falls to the ground, and his adversary makes the mistake of thinking it's over. Then about the time we've relaxed in our padded theater seats and celebration is commencing on-screen, the "dead" person suddenly reappears, not quite as dead as we had thought.

Satan hates to be surprised like that. So just because our lives have turned upside-down, just because we have fallen, doesn't mean he stops shooting. Not at all.

Just when we are the most disoriented, he steps up the fight. The ferocity of our enemy is similar to that of an angry mob. The Academy Award-winning movie *Black Hawk Down* retells the true story of an elite group of American Rangers and Delta Force soldiers who are sent into Somalia in 1993 to capture an evil warlord. When the mission goes terribly wrong, they suddenly find themselves in a bloody firefight. In one of the scenes a soldier, fighting for his life, is wounded and trapped in his downed helicopter. Running low on ammo and surrounded by hundreds of armed rioters, he does his best to fight back, but there are just too many guns. After being repeatedly shot, his dead body is hoisted like a trophy over the celebrating mob.

THE HEROIC PATH

Satan has the same hatred for us. It's true that we may have made some mistakes that landed us where we are, some critical mistakes. I'm not trying to excuse our behavior or diminish our sin. But our enemy is not done with us when we're down, and he typically uses people to finish us off. The crowd arrives like a pack of hungry wolves, accusing us, attacking our already broken lives. And they aren't necessarily wrong in doing so; they may simply be defending their own land and lives.

After my affair, it was important for my wife to vent her pain and frustration, and I needed to let her do so. But in the course of that process, Satan tried to convince me that it would never end, and brought multiple waves of attack.

The onslaught became tremendously disheartening. When the details of my failure became common knowledge and my wife and I separated for a while, our children were all attending a private Christian school. Just stepping out of my truck to pick them up from their classes felt more like I was jumping out of a U-boat at Omaha Beach on D-Day than walking onto a schoolyard. I felt every arrow when people stared at me and then looked away when I caught their glances. The shame was almost unbearable.

Worse yet was knowing that my children felt it too. My daughter, who was thirteen at the time, understood exactly what had happened. I could see her friends running up to her, hugging and crying with her. I was grateful that she had such good friends; yet I knew I was the one who had caused the pain that elicited their care. Those experiences were more than bullets;

they were grenades dropped right into my foxhole. The shrapnel left me bleeding, disoriented, and wishing for a quick end to my miserable existence.

Work really was not much of an escape either. Since the woman I had been involved with had worked with me, my office likewise became just another battlefield. I became depressed, unable to talk or interact with other employees. My work suffered. Every minute seemed to drag on and on. My only solace was a good friend, who in a very non-judgmental way allowed me to move into his home. There I found a place of cease-fire and refuge.

I share this part of my story not to gain your pity, but to bring to light the immensity of the battle. When men fall, especially to moral failure, it can become very difficult to find any allies. It is here that we must be men and learn to fight to the end. And what I mean by fighting is fighting for our hearts.

A lot of us fight for our lives instead of our hearts, just trying to survive. As the onslaught continues, our self-preservation instinct kicks in and we respond much like a cornered cat. We begin lashing out, trying to clear some space and looking for a tree that we can escape to and hide in. That is exactly where our enemy wants us: all by ourselves, trapped up in a tree.

The Real Battle

Proverbs 4:23 says, "Above all else, guard your heart, for it is the wellspring of life." It is in this place, the place where we have fallen, that we must guard our hearts because it is here that Satan wants to finish what he has started and take our hearts out. Not content to see us fall, he wants to assure that we never get up again.

If you have experienced the devastation of sexual sin, you know exactly what I am referring to. It doesn't have to be an affair. It may have just been some pictures, fantasies, perhaps an inappropriate emotional relationship; or it may have been much darker, finding yourself in the world of prostitution or homosexuality. Jesus says it's all the same. And our enemy uses it to produce the same results: the shame and accusations of others and from within to take you out of the story.

That was Satan's plan all along. Sure, he is happy if your marriage fails or your ministry is discredited, but he doesn't stop there. He has a much more sinister plan. He wants you off the field and out of the battle completely. I wish I could promise you that your family will be okay or that you will bear no consequences for your sin, but I can't. I know all too well the carnage caused by my own failures. What I can promise you, though, is that God isn't finished with you. You still have a role to play in His story.

That is why your heart feels assaulted even years after the event and why sensuality can become a lifelong battle. Our hearts are the wellspring of life, the essence of our new lives in Christ. As such, it is our hearts, not just our honor, that Satan desires to destroy. It is critical that we understand the difference. Too often we equate the two, but they are not the same.

Your honor may have been defamed and even destroyed by your sin, but your heart has not been. If you are in Christ—which is to say, if you are a Christian—then you are "a new creation; the old has gone, and the new has come!" (2 Corinthians 5:17). Even if you are, at this moment, daily browsing pornographic sites or continuing an inappropriate relationship, your behavior is not the truest representation of who you are.

With our "I can do it" attitude, we men typically evaluate our problem and conclude that we simply need to try harder. So we pull up our bootstraps and redouble our efforts. Yet despite our efforts, we find ourselves once again in the same place: running for our lives, or failing to engage with those around us, or just looking for a new distraction. In the daily assault, our hearts take the most hits, which is why the writer of Proverbs tells us to guard them.

If you have found yourself taken out by sexual sin, then your heart is at risk. Paul emphasizes this truth in 1 Corinthians 6, where he states that we are to flee from sexual immorality (v. 18). Paul explains that all other sins are committed outside of the body, but sexual sins are committed against our own bodies, which are temples of the Holy Spirit, homes for the very heart of Christ.

If you've been overtaken by sexual sin, then you know how it plays out. First comes the sin. But it never stops there. Shame and accusation begin paying us regular visits. Satan loves this part of the attack. Having engineered our fall in the first place, our Accuser immediately strikes a second and a third blow. Through our own self-recrimination or the condemnation of others, he replays our failures before us. In doing so, he uses the same words that he used with Eve: "Did God really say?"

"Did God really say that you are a new creation? Did God really say that Christ now lives in you? Did God really say that He would never leave you? Look at yourself. Look at your shame. His words cannot be true."

What Is Truth?

At this point, many men begin to question whether there is any good in them. And if they conclude that there is not … well, the options become quite limited. The easiest alternative is to just give in to the man they have become. "Why fight it, it is just who I am."

I hope that you are beginning to see this. It is exactly the position the Enemy hopes men will take. From here, the rest of his job is easy. "If this is who I really am," we think, "then why not go back there again?" Why not just give up on marriage—or any relationship, for that matter? Why not view women as trophies of a hard day's work? Why not walk away from the life that Christ has for us? If we are just hopeless sinners with the vilest of behavior, then the truth of the Scriptures must not be so true after all.

"But you were washed," Paul argues, "you were sanctified, you were justified in the name of the Lord Jesus Christ and by the Spirit of our God" (1 Corinthians 6:11). Notice that Paul writes this in the past tense. It is a done deal; it is not something that is being accomplished by our efforts, but rather, it is something that Jesus consummated once and completely. "It is finished," Jesus proclaimed before breathing His last on the cross. What is true of you is true because of Him, not your sins.

This is why G1, the girls, can be so toxic to a man. The lust of the flesh promises something of God, something of beauty

G1: The Girls

and compassion and ecstasy, and then delivers just the opposite: a denial of the power and work of God. And we are living in a world that actively promotes both messages. It truly is a war zone. You cannot turn on the computer or the television, or even drive down the road, without encountering calls from the false god of sexual temptation. G1 is intoxicating, overwhelming. It has taken many good men out. If you, like me, have been shot down and ambushed, then you have likely also questioned God's power. You have endured shame and ostracism and have seriously doubted that God could ever use you again.

To you I say, now is the time to begin fighting for your heart again. The writer of Hebrews reminds us that God's words are as true today as they have been for thousands of years. "Therefore God again set a certain day, calling it Today, when a long time later he spoke through David, as was said before: 'Today, if you hear his voice, do not harden your hearts'" (Hebrews 4:7). It is easy to lose heart in this battle. But God longs to stand with you in the midst of the chaos to preserve, heal, and strengthen your heart.

I never want to minimize the seriousness and the consequences of our failings. Amends need to be made. True repentance, which involves turning from our sin, is essential. But these things are not enough. Men are created to engage the Enemy, to press forward and take his territory. We are created in the warrior image of our God, and when we shrink from that image and retreat, we not only lose a battle, we risk losing the entire war.

The good news is this:

THE HEROIC PATH

As we begin to understand how and why our enemy attacks …
as we recognize who we are in Christ …
and as we discover what our place is in God's story …
then the situations that Satan has used to harm us and those around us become opportunities for God to do what God does so well: redeem us and accomplish His great purpose for our lives.

TRAIL MARKERS

1. Close your eyes for moment and think of women. What thoughts or images appear? How do they represent the God-created wonder of a woman? How have they been poisoned and distorted by the culture we live in?
2. Embarrassment, accusations, shame, and a sense of disqualification from God's calling: I struggled with them all as a result of my personal indiscretion. What has been your own experience if you, like me, have lived in the shadow of a sexual sin?
3. Have you ever experienced the "crowds turning against you"? What did it feel like? How did you respond?
4. Many believe that "the heart is desperately evil" even after a person accepts Christ. Read 2 Corinthians 5:17. What does that say about who you really are? Why *do* you or *don't* you believe that your new heart is still evil?
5. How does sexual sin attack the identity of who you are in Christ? How might you effectively respond to such an attack?
6. If you have struggled in the area of sexual integrity, consider praying this prayer: Jesus, thank You for redeeming me and making me a new creation. I acknowledge Your heart living in me and the completeness of Your work in me. Forgive me for my sexual failings as well as for my small faith in the sufficiency of what You have accomplished in me. I claim now Your blood over all that I am, and by Your authority I break any agreements that I have made with my enemy concerning who I am. I want to be wholly Yours. I once again take my place as a son of the King, set apart for Your purpose. Amen

Chapter Four

G2: The Gold

There are people who have money and people who are rich.

Coco Chanel

"Meaningless! Meaningless!" says the Teacher.
"Utterly meaningless! Everything is meaningless."
What does a man gain from all his labor
at which he toils under the sun?

Ecclesiastes 1:2–3

THE HEROIC PATH

Adolph Merckle was the ninety-fourth richest man in the world in 2008 according to Forbes.com.[4] His worth: 9.2 billion dollars! A native of Dresden, Germany, Merckle was a brilliant investor and a passionate family man. Taking the reins of his grandfather's chemical wholesale company, he turned it into one of the largest pharmaceutical manufacturers in the world.

As if that weren't enough, Merckle also built a massive concrete supply company, acquiring smaller companies until he became a global player in the building materials market. He owned stock in a multitude of other companies as well. Called the Warren Buffet of Germany, in 2005 Merckle was awarded the *Bundesverdienstkreuz* (Federal Cross of Merit), his country's highest decoration.

Then in 2008, Adolph Merckle made a bold and dangerous assessment of the European auto industry. Speculating on the then-volatile Volkswagen auto maker's stock, he engaged in an investment strategy known as short selling in which he borrowed a large number of shares in the Volkswagen Company and then immediately sold them, hoping they would decrease in value and he could buy them back. Instead, the auto giant Porsche secured controlling interest in Volkswagen, and its stock skyrocketed.

Mr. Merckle lost hundreds of millions of dollars. Distraught and feeling hopeless, he threw himself in front of a train near his villa in the German hamlet of Blaubeuren on January 4, 2009. Mr. Merckle was seventy-four years old. Gold, riches, wealth—call it whatever you want, there is something about the allure of money that draws men.

---

4 Luisa Kroll, "The World's Billionaires," Forbes: www.forbes.com (March 5, 2008).

G2: The Gold

On January 24, 1848, James W. Marshall discovered gold at Sutter's Mill in Coloma, California. Over the next few years, over 300,000 people rushed to California in search of riches, often at great risk to self and family. The California Gold Rush became a sort of icon to the American dream, a deep-seated belief that if we are willing to work hard and risk much, our dreams can come true.

I am not condemning this idea nor the pursuit of wealth, and I don't believe the Word of God condemns them. Many godly men are quite wealthy, men whom I would do well to emulate. Further, in examining the Scriptures, we find God blessing Old-Testament figures such as Jacob, Abraham, Job, and David with earthly riches. And the New Testament mentions people who had the financial means to help support Jesus's ministry.

Paul the apostle has often been misquoted as saying that money is the root of all sin. He never said that; rather he warned that "the love of money is a root of all kinds of evil" (1 Timothy 6:10). There is a vast difference between those two statements. This being said, there is a great danger in the "love of money" that Paul refers to.

It is the second G, the Gold, that we will examine in this chapter.

Let's face it, we all could use more money. Our society and our economy depend on money. We need it to feed our families, send our children to school, and purchase the healthcare required in order to maintain our bodies.

Without cash, I wouldn't have clothes to wear, a bed to sleep in, or a computer to write with. Even some expendable cash is important; all work and no play certainly does make Jack a dull boy, and a rather shallow one at that. Perhaps more than anything else, I value the family vacations, date nights with my wife, and "toys" for my children (okay, me too) that my money purchases. These things are a large part of my sanity. So yes, I admit it: I love money. In the words of screen star Bo Derek, "Whoever said money can't buy happiness simply didn't know where to go shopping."

The Pursuit of Happiness

The problem comes when the love of money consumes us, when our days become driven by the pursuit of money. That can happen so easily. Most of us, even the Adolph Merckles of the world, don't start our lives with the acquisition of wealth as our driving force. Usually the lust for money begins with more virtuous motives: a better life for our family; a desire to retire early and invest our life in altruistic pursuits; or maybe just a God-given desire to be our best, working with all of our heart as if working for the Lord.

Yet too often, something shifts. Maybe the better life that we dreamed of for our family has become too much to maintain. Or some risk we took didn't pan out, and now we find ourselves struggling not merely to retire early, but to retire at all.

Even if our efforts work out well, success can become a very jealous mistress in herself. Sugar Ray Leonard, the famed boxer from the 1980s, once noted, "Although it was a great accomplishment to win a Gold medal, once they put it on you, that's it; your career is over." In other words, there's no place to go now but down. So you're driven to keep on top of your game, to win at all costs.

That is how the love of money becomes the root of all kinds of evil. Our enemy uses it as a foothold in our lives, holding us just below the surface of the water where we struggle to get a breath. We become consumed with the fight to get on top and stay on top. For men especially, money has a lure that is hard to resist. We measure ourselves by how well we keep up with the Joneses. And even if we don't subscribe to that value, we sense that everyone else does.

Perhaps more than anything else, money offers a tangible measure of our success as men. Yes, we all say that there are more important and reliable measures such as friends, family, and health. But such things are difficult to quantify and flaunt. Nice clothes, fast cars, big homes—those are the things that speak of our accomplishments the loudest and to the greatest number of people.

Perhaps that is why the rich young ruler in the gospels went away sad. Matthew, Mark, and Luke all tell his story. He was a man of great wealth and position. Yet despite his riches, he apparently felt unsatisfied. We are told by Mark that he ran up and literally threw himself at the feet of the itinerant preacher named Jesus. This young ruler had a burning question: "What must I do to inherit eternal life?" (Mark 10:17). He needed to know, and somehow he realized that Jesus was the only one who could tell him.

Heart Surgery

What a great question! What a vital question! It really is *the* question that all of us at some point want to ask, *need* to ask. The Master's answer was rather perplexing for those of us who understand grace, but for this man, it was brilliant. Jesus basically tells him to obey the Ten Commandments.

Now, this man was a mover and shaker. He was likely a type-A personality through and through. When it came to keeping the Law, he had done so. Probably not perfectly, but he had worked harder at it than most. So he asked, "Is there anything else?" Maybe he knew he was still missing something. Or maybe he expected Jesus to say, "No, that's it, you've done it. You've arrived dude. Way to go!"

We understand, though, that Jesus isn't interested in our vain efforts. No, He is much more concerned about our hearts. Mark goes on: "Jesus looked at him and loved him. 'One thing you lack,' he said. 'Go, sell everything you have and give to the poor, and you will have treasure in heaven. Then come, follow me'" (Mark 10:21).

"Jesus looked at him and loved him." I love that! Christianity has sadly become a religion more of hate than love these days. We hate the abortionist, the immoral, the liar, the thief, and certainly the greedy. Jesus doesn't. He loves imperfect people, and he loved this man. Jesus loved him so much that He wanted to reveal to the man what his pursuit of wealth had done to him, how far it had taken him from the passions of his youth. Passions the man no doubt thought he still had. Passion above all to pursue God.

So Jesus explained that there was just one more thing the young ruler needed to do: sell everything and follow Him.

Understand, Jesus was not being legalistic. Just the opposite. He was inviting the man to walk away from the need to prove himself and instead trust the leading of the King. What an incredible invitation—unless, of course, the young ruler had no real interest in trusting Jesus to lead him; unless he preferred to be his own master, make his own future, be his own boss.

Let's face it, we're no different. We'd rather chart our own courses. We want to prove that we have what it takes, that we've "made it." We love to flaunt our possessions, thereby proving to the naysayers—and perhaps more importantly, to ourselves—that we really are something.

Thus, when we fail on the financial front—when, like Adolph Merckle, we lose it all or maybe never attain it in the first place—then our very identity as a man is challenged. Even if we know in our head that worldly wealth is not the true measure of who we are, the verdict of our society is one of unimaginable shame.

The Search for Significance

Financial failure doesn't have to be catastrophic to affect us. The experience of a temporary layoff or a decrease in our standard of living can equally shake us. We live in an optimistic time when most of us believe that tomorrow will be better, and by "better," we usually mean financially better. This conviction can lead us to some pretty devastating conclusions when the future begins to look less than bright. Since we think it should get progressively better, then somehow we must be to blame when it turns out otherwise. When the search for significance becomes intertwined with monetary success, then the drive to succeed financially will either affirm us or ruin us and perhaps even kill us.

Of course, not all men struggle financially. Consider the man who has done well for himself. He has worked hard, sacrificed much, and been rewarded richly. He is living the American Dream with fine clothes, fast cars, and his own ornate castle on the hill. Moreover, he is a good man. But the very goodness in him ultimately leads him to a sobering realization: all that he has accumulated has never produced any lasting satisfaction, and his financial achievements have failed to buy him true significance. Like the man who has never "made it," this man, too, finds himself looking in the mirror and wondering how he could have failed so greatly.

Part of man's curse at the fall was, "By the sweat of your brow you will eat your food" (Genesis 3:19). In other words, obtaining food—or, by extension, obtaining the wealth required to provide life's essentials—will forever be a struggle. The quest for wealth will take all that we are as men, and it will have the power to consume us. It can even kill us. But that deadly power is not from God; it is a product of the fall. And the good news is this: death is what Jesus has come to raise us from.

From Death to Life

As our Lord entered Jerusalem during the final week before His crucifixion, He began to spell out for His followers the tenets of the new kingdom He was ushering in. "I tell you the truth, unless a kernel of wheat falls to the ground and dies, it remains only a single seed. But if it dies, it produces many seeds. The man who loves his life will lose it, while the man who hates his life in this world will keep it for eternal life. Whoever serves me must follow me; and where I am, my servant also will be" (John 12:24–26).

That was the good news Jesus was offering to the rich young ruler: Neither the man's riches nor the lack thereof needed to define him. Jesus was inviting him into something of much greater worth.

I know that we know this, but we need to KNOW it in the deepest part of our being. Paul, as he is praying for the Christians in Ephesus, says that he is praying that they would "know [the] love that surpasses knowledge" (Ephesians 3:19). What is this knowing? It is the intimacy of discovery. It is the kind of knowing that a man has of his wife, which he only finds in the marriage bed when they are naked and unashamed and there is nothing left to hide behind. It is the knowing that can only happen when all of our false selves, all of our self-built monuments to our own significance, are torn down. This type of knowing cannot be obtained by study or contemplation or even prayer, but rather must be experienced and walked through.

I believe this is why the Bible frequently addresses the issue of riches and the giving away of riches to God and to others. We may say that everything we own belongs to God, but come on, we worked for it—by the sweat of our brow, I might add! Losing it, or not having enough of it, or simply realizing that we have wasted so much of our lives obtaining it, can feel like death. That's why men jump from windows on Wall Street. They're not killing themselves; they are already dead. They are just closing the books. If you have been to the point of realizing how little you can depend on wealth while at the same time wanting to do so, you know exactly what I mean.

I am intrigued, if not a little irritated, by how our Enemy often attacks me in the very area that I am teaching on. These past few weeks, while writing this chapter, I have experienced such an attack. My wife and I have made some choices concerning our children's education that have stretched us financially. We have also felt called by God to learn what it means to give sacrificially.

Both of these challenges plus our usual expenses plus the impact of our country's economic downturn all came to a head a few weeks ago. Not for the first time, we had more bills than cash at the end of the month. And that's when I learned that my salary would likely decrease in the coming year.

You can say that you trust God all you want to during such times, but truthfully, I was in a panic. "How are we going to make it? What else can we cut?" And of course, the big one, "God, I thought You said that You would provide!" I felt exposed as the failed provider I always knew I was. I began scheming, planning, manipulating. I grew irritable, my prayer life became much quieter, and I honestly questioned whether God had indeed called me to anything in his kingdom.

On top of all that, it was tax season, and I needed to meet with my accountant to prepare our yearly return.

Thankfully, I have a number of good men who walk with me, men who saw my fears and doubts. I shared my frustrations with them, and many of them began praying for me.

G2: The Gold

When I met with my tax accountant and he finished my return, he announced that I would actually receive a whopping $53 refund. Well, at least I didn't owe any more money. That was a good thing!

Then I asked my accountant about a message he had sent me a few months back inquiring about a possible unreported business expense. He didn't remember the message, but he called in a partner to review my records. Sure enough, there was the expense! And not only could I claim it this year, I could actually go back and claim it for previous years. The result would be a refund of almost $15,000! I nearly fell on the floor.

What struck me most about the whole experience was not how faithfully God provided for my needs (and probably more than a few wants), but rather how quickly I doubted God and His plan for me when the money wasn't there. My position as a provider and producer defined my identity to a surprising degree, and I too easily agreed with my enemy concerning my worth as a person during those days.

I wish I could promise that God would provide a sudden windfall for you like He did for me. I can't. I could share many times when the financial blessings didn't materialize for me either. What I can tell you, though, is that God knows about men's financial fears and how they take you and me out of the battle. His heart is to invite us back into the story, offering us true life in Himself. As with the rich young ruler, Jesus never looks at us in contempt. Rather, he views us with love and a genuine concern for where each of us is personally in relation to the passion He birthed in us to pursue Him.

THE HEROIC PATH

I know you remember that passion. Quite possibly it has reawakened in you recently. Passion for God and His kingdom explains why you are reading this book right now. So listen: Jesus is extending an invitation to you, not necessarily to give all that you own to the poor, but rather to remember—and then to follow.

TRAIL MARKERS

1. Do you know someone who has used money either well or not so well? Why do you think he was a good or poor steward of his finances?
2. In your own pursuit of wealth and financial security, what choices have you made that you feel are honorable?
3. Have you ever felt as if the pursuit of wealth got out of hand and possibly become a distraction to your walk with Jesus? How so?
4. In what ways and to what degree do you derive a sense of personal significance from your job and your ability to acquire wealth?
5. How might God be using your issues with money to draw you into the full life that He has for you.

Chapter Five

G3: The Glory

*Our greatest glory is not in never failing,
but in rising every time we fail.*

Ralph Waldo Emerson

Vanity of vanities, saith the preacher; all is vanity.

Ecclesiastes 12:8 KJV

THE HEROIC PATH

Jacob (not his real name) grew up way too fast. His mother was a drug addict and his father … well Jacob doesn't talk about his father, isn't sure he ever knew the man. Jacob's best memories of his childhood were formed with his grandfather. Thanks to him, Jacob found a place in a church and excelled in school. During those times with Grandfather, life seemed somewhat normal.

They weren't enough, though. In a neighborhood cluttered with crime and violence, Jacob in his early teens began seeking his identity in drugs, alcohol, and street gangs. When his grandfather died, Jacob, like so many lost men (be they thirteen or thirty), looked for his place in life through those around him.

Call the third G what you will—peer pressure, narcissism, self-identity, or what the Scriptures says it is: "the boasting of what [a man] has and does" (1 John 2:16)—the quest for glory is what drove Jacob. And it didn't just drive him, it consumed him. Jacob's friends gave him the nickname "Wicked," and by his own account, wicked is exactly what Jacob became.

Jacob joined an inner-city gang, an organized crime syndicate. Drinking binges, cocaine, and paint-huffing became the mainstays of his days—all by his fifteenth birthday. The instability at home led Jacob to set out on his own. He slept in abandoned buildings, stole cars, and robbed homes to support his escalating drug habits and to buy food.

Yet one thing was still true of this young teenager, just as it is of all men: Jacob desperately longed to "be the man"—to have those around him view him as important and powerful, someone to be respected. Like you and me, Jacob longed for glory.

G3: The Glory

His chance to attain it finally came one night: an opportunity for Jacob to prove that he was the baddest, the meanest, the wickedest. A rival gang had started something and Jacob's gang wanted payback. Driving through the other gang's territory, they spied a couple of their enemies in front of a home. With their vehicle's lights out, Jacob and his friends cruised slowly by. Then Jacob, literally riding shotgun, raised the 20-gauge he had with him and began shooting.

Shouting, screaming, chaos … it was all over in a few seconds. Jacob's shots had found a victim. "Wicked" began bragging to his buddies. He had lived up to his nickname. He really was wicked, and for a gang member, such a reputation can be an intoxicating glory.

Jacob and his homies were long gone when the police arrive. What the officers found was not a murdered gang member but an eight-year-old boy, shot in the head. Playing innocently in his front yard, he had become the victim of a young man's drive for glory.

As for Jacob, at an age when most boys should be dreaming of homecoming dances and catching the winning touchdown pass, he was arrested, tried, and sentenced to life in prison. It's difficult for me to comprehend how anyone could have such utter disregard for the life of another human being. How can one person willingly destroy others for just a few moments of glory?

Yet, if I am honest, I must admit that I am not all that different from Jacob. Part of my curse, the curse of all men from the fall, is that I must forever produce by the sweat of my brow.

Whether our field is corn, cars, cash, or conquests, something in men responds aggressively to the challenge to produce. We will attain whatever it is we're after by whatever means necessary, and damn the consequences. That's the attitude we men have been taught from our youth, and it is a value that comes straight from the pit of hell. While it may not cause us to poke a shotgun out of a car window, it can and does lead us to drive our agendas past innocent bystanders, stepping on whoever may get in our way, irrespective of who gets hurt in the process.

The Temptation for Glory

Don't get me wrong. I'm by no means saying that ambition and success are innately wrong. I believe that God wants us to give our best to honorable pursuits.

Paul the apostle taught that if a man did not work, he should not eat, and it is a gross oversimplification to equate the desires of a drug-addled gang member with the ambitions of a man trying to provide for his family. I personally have aspirations and dreams, good ones, ones that I believe God wants me to reach for, and I'm sure you have dreams of your own.

Yet as we pursue our God-given desires, our Lord warns us to be "shrewd as snakes and as innocent as doves" (Matthew 10:16). The reason, He explains, is because He is sending us out among wolves. We may be going out with the best intentions, but someone out there is determined to take us off course.

Satan tempted even Jesus with the third G. We are told that before Jesus began his public ministry, He went out into the desert for forty days of fasting. At the end of that period, when Jesus was tired, hungry, and, as any true man, quite likely beginning to experience the weightiness of his mission, Satan attacked with three final temptations. Luke describes one of them in this manner: The devil led Him to Jerusalem and had Him stand on the highest point of the temple. "If you are the Son of God," he said, "throw yourself down from here. For it is written: 'He will command his angels concerning you to guard you carefully; they will lift you up in their hands, so that you will not strike your foot against a stone'" (Luke 4:9–11).

What strikes me about this temptation is how silly it sounds. I mean, really? Throw yourself down from the temple? Sounds like some teenage YouTube dare. However, when we consider what Jesus was preparing to do—establish Himself as the Messiah, the Savior of the world—and as we recognize that the temple was where all of the religious big shots hung out, then this temptation makes more sense. Satan was offering Jesus a sure way to establish His credibility. In front of everyone, publicly, Jesus would fulfill the promise of an Old Testament psalm and thereby prove He was the real deal. There was just one problem: this was not the path His Father had laid out for Him. Yes, it would have won Him glory and greatness; and yes, many would likely have believed in Him as a result. But Jesus sought something higher than human adulation; He sought His Father's will.

Remember: we are to be as shrewd as snakes and innocent as doves. Trying to manipulate our glory and thus bypass God's path for us does nothing more than lead us down a dark street, headlights off, with shotgun in hand, as we attempt to create our own destiny.

THE HEROIC PATH

Shrewdness and Innocence

To be shrewd is to be astute, keen, discerning. Like a snake, we are to know our objective while remaining alert to danger. Shrewdness requires focus and a constant tasting of the air.

We men often fail to behave shrewdly in our pursuits. Having started with honorable intentions, we grow restless when results don't arrive as quickly or as consistently as we had hoped. As any good coach would do, we reassess the situation. Perhaps we discover that our approach was misdirected or that we had read our opportunities incorrectly. Something must change; after all, we've all heard that insanity is doing the same thing over and over while expecting different results, right?

So when what seem to be reasonable solutions appear, we forget to stop and test the air. Something shifts as we begin to smell victory, and our shrewdness collapses. We charge ahead, jumping from the top of the temple in a desperate attempt to make our mark.

The worst part is that sometimes it works. We hit pay dirt; we make the winning shot and the crowd goes wild. Few things speak as loudly to a man as applause. Acclaim can be intoxicating, and once you have experienced it, it can quickly become your drug of choice. This is the "boasting of what [a man] has and does" that John warns us about. We've all read the stories or seen the headlines of the Hollywood star or the Hall of Famer who became obsessed with power, thinking himself or herself above even the law. What started as a noble and talented career morphed into deception and manipulation, all in an attempt to maintain the power-high.

G3: The Glory

However, Jesus not only warns us to be as shrewd as serpents. He also tells us to be as innocent as doves, a significantly harder task on some days. When opportunities arise that demand instant action, it's easy to step on those who seem to slow us down. And the people we walk over are often the very ones we least want to hurt.

Last night I rented a copy of the 2008 film *The Hurt Locker*. It is a poignant picture, following one of the U.S. Army's elite EOD (Explosive Ordnance Disposal) teams as it searched for and disarmed IEDs (improvised explosive devices) during the Iraqi war. The jobs of these brave men brought them face-to-face with the daily possibility of death. But with that risk, also came a similar level of glory.

Jeremy Renner plays Sergeant First Class William James, a reckless, unorthodox cowboy who regularly puts his company in harm's way. However, he is also very good at what he does, and as a result, many lives are saved. Sergeant James earns the respect of his comrades, and perhaps more significantly, fills a void left in his character by his inability to connect on other levels.

As the movie progresses, we find that Sergeant James has a wife and young son, both of whom he loves and misses. However, as his tour finally ends and he finds himself at home again with his family, James confesses to his infant son that there is only one thing that he truly loves. In the next scene we see him stepping off a plane to begin another 365-day tour, a grin of satisfaction and belonging written across his face.

The movie begins with a quote by war correspondent Chris Hedges stating that "war is a drug." But it's not just war that is a drug. In its myriad forms, glory intoxicates and addicts men. Like

THE HEROIC PATH

Sergeant James, we too can find ourselves leaving those who are most important to us in the background as we search for our next taste of glory. Like a drug addict looking for his next high, we need to hear the applause again … and again … and again.

Most successful men have this craving for glory in them to a large degree, be they pastors, doctors, CEOs, or professional athletes. The quest for glory is what drives us men. It is likely what drove Churchill to save the free world, Michael Jordan to dominate basketball, and more than a few ministry leaders to touch the lives of millions of souls.

Unfortunately, as we review the front pages of our local newspaper, we find that it is also what has brought down more than a few good men. World leaders, athletes, executives, and even pastors can quickly find themselves in over their heads in ventures that are far easier to get into than they are to get out of. Perhaps you've had such an experience yourself. It can happen far too quickly and subtly. One minute you are pursuing a dream; the next, your dream has become a nightmare.

Exposed

Nightmares are strange experiences. Some nightmares are absolutely terrifying. You find yourself running for your life, or trying frantically to get above water, or screaming an inaudible, silent shriek. But other nightmares are much more subtle. You may be the hero, giving the big speech or receiving some honor, only to look down and realize that you forgot to put your pants on

G3: The Glory

that morning. Most men live with a fear of this kind of exposure: being found out, their glory shamed.

It is devastating to have our most personal failures brought to light—the ones that reflect directly on our character. A man who harms those he loves or even his own reputation on the way to success is the most broken of all men. How does one recover from such selfishness? If a man steals money, he can give it back. If he has an affair, he can break it off. But if he destroys his reputation by stepping on those who love him, the repair process can take decades, and complete recovery may never occur.

Even the process of repair can be fraught with danger, becoming just another project, another goal to accomplish. Many men finally conclude that there really is no greater success available for them in this life, and so, disillusioned and addicted, they go back to what they know—another tour of duty, disarming bombs, risking limbs ... and missing life.

Of the Three Gs, this one haunts me the most. I love to succeed, to look great. I love the feeling of mastering something, the satisfaction I get when I accomplish a feat few others can boast of. But I also know that this drive in me probably causes more strife in my marriage than any other issue. My wife feels lonely; she says I'm not engaged. My kids act out or become just as distant as I am. It's that whole "Cat's in the Cradle" thing: they'll grow up just like me.

All of this is really the last thing I want. I love my family very much. I'd give my life for them, and I want to be a source of joy and friendship to each of them. Yet I also have my own needs and my own callings. Giving up the pursuits I love in order to please them will have just the opposite effect. I'll feel resentful and they'll feel guilty.

However, I also fear being the kind of man who lies one day on his death bed, alone. Having accomplished much, he has really lost much more. This is perhaps the ultimate failure: To come to the end of our lives and realize that we missed it. To recognize too late that in our quest to be seen as the best or the baddest—or just be seen, period—we, like sixteen-year-old Jacob, injured innocent lives. And in so doing, we sentenced ourselves to a life term in a prison of our own making.

That is the truly damning part of the third G, and most of us sense its viper-like presence. We can almost taste its venom. Like a hungry serpent, our enemy, Satan, feeds off of our fear even as he convinces us to rationalize our latest self-serving enterprise.

"It is only for a season," he tells us. Once we have accomplished the next step, we'll be done. We know it's not true, but still we listen. It's easier than changing.

Or we hear, "You are never going to change. It's just the way you are. In fact, your family should be thankful that you have accomplished so much." I almost laugh as I write that—or maybe cry, as those thoughts have entered my own head so many times. There is, of course, a hint of truth in them. I am largely who I am as a result of the drives that I have. Those drives are not all bad; many of them are from God, and He intends me to pursue them. But here is the kicker: in pursuing my drives, I have a responsibility to administer them as well.

G3: The Glory

I love the Lord's Prayer. It begins by addressing our Father in Heaven. And that is how we must begin this journey of walking in the battle and living with our failures: by walking in intimacy with our heavenly Father. It certainly isn't a matter of ignoring who we are and trying to become someone we are not. Yet, neither is it okay, or even sane, for us to disregard our shortcomings, our indiscretions and narcissisms, and proceed as if consequences don't matter. Between the two extremes is a place of balance found only when we present ourselves in our entirety to our Father, hiding nothing, confident of His leading.

You see, the wonder of the first line of the Lord's Prayer lies in what it implies: we are sons of the King. Paul said it this way: "But you did not receive a spirit that makes you a slave again to fear, but you received the Spirit of sonship. And by him we cry, '*Abba*, Father'" (Romans 8:15).

As sons, we are invited to sit at the table of the King, to learn from Him, to be fathered by Him. Doing His will is not so much a matter of changing who we are, but rather of learning to walk with Christ as the individuals He created us to be, with all of our ambitions and desires and drives.

TRAIL MARKERS

1. What are some of the "glories" you have pursued, either honorable or dishonorable?
2. In what ways has your glory been like a drug?
3. Who has experienced the greatest pain from your addiction?
4. What has been your response to their pain? Have you just given up and abandoned all of your dreams? Or do you lean toward the opposite extreme, figuring that "you can't please everyone, so you might as well please yourself"?
5. Do you feel that it is possible to pursue your dreams and desires while avoiding the pitfalls of pride and narcissism? How would it affect you to have God fathering you through that journey?

Chapter Six

World at War

Toto, I have a feeling we're not in Kansas anymore.

Dorothy in *The Wizard of Oz*

Dear friends, do not be surprised at the painful trial you are suffering, as though something strange were happening to you.

1 Peter 4:12

THE HEROIC PATH

The scene is the heart of the Mediterranean Sea. It's the middle of the night, and, in a fishing boat tossing back and forth on the rough water, half-a-dozen fishermen are passing the time with a game of poker. Another man, making his rounds on deck, notices something bobbing amid the waves. He looks again, focuses his eyes in the darkness, and recognizes the body of a man. Under a radiant moon, the men hoist the corpse on deck with fishing hooks, assuming him to be dead.

But he is not. This mysterious man floating in the center of the ocean is somehow alive—barely, but alive just the same. He has bullet holes in his body; he is wearing some kind of military uniform; and he has a coded message embedded under his skin. Upon awakening, the bewildered guest has no idea who he is, where he is, or how he got there. Dehydrated, disoriented, and amnesiac, Jason Bourne finds himself caught up in a war of which he has no knowledge or recollection. And he is the primary target.

The Bourne Identity could just as easily be called Our Identity, though many of us, much like Matt Damon's character early in the movie, have yet to put the pieces together. Disoriented and confused, we too are amnesiac of our true identity and likewise are genuinely surprised that anyone would want to harm us. What have we done? Why would we be targeted? There must be some mistake.

Yet if we follow the clues and pay attention to the strange yet somehow familiar thoughts that press through the fog, some startling facts about our existence start piecing together.

Sheep among Wolves

Most of us walk through life with a rather naïve view of the world. The washing machine that decides to flood the house hours before our long awaited family vacation; the date night that out of nowhere turns into a fight night; the resistance of those closest to us as we follow a lifelong dream—we tend to view such things as just bad luck: doo-doo happens.

Recognizing that we live in an imperfect world, we may develop a sort of pessimistic apathy: nothing ever works out anyway. Worse, we may blame God, convinced that He must be disappointed with us.

But then we discover a clue—not in a laser message embedded under our skin, but in a book of ancient writings sitting on the back corner of our bed stand.

Journey with me back through time to a key moment in the tenth chapter of Matthew's gospel. Moments before Jesus sends his twelve closest associates on their first training mission, He gives them "authority to drive out evil spirits and to heal every disease and sickness" (v. 1). Jesus next commands them, "Preach this message: 'The kingdom of heaven is near.' Heal the sick, raise the dead, cleanse those who have leprosy, drive out demons." (vv. 7–8).

Now, these are the same twelve who had been with Jesus as He turned water into wine, restored sight to the blind, and even raised the daughter of one of the local Jewish leaders from the dead. They have seen Him confront the religious zealots of their day with boldness and wrath while offering hope to those who had been

THE HEROIC PATH

discarded by society. I can just imagine Peter talking to his fellow disciples. "Oh, this is gonna be good, guys! Can you imagine? We're going to be doing what Jesus did! Did you hear Him? He gave us authority. No more sitting around being nobodies—this is the real deal. We are going to kick some demon butt!"

But suddenly Jesus changes His tone. "I am sending you out like sheep among wolves" (v. 16). *What?* Peter cleans his ears. "He must have meant that He is sending us out like wolves among sheep, right? We're the predators now—aren't we?"

Jesus continues, "Be on your guard against men; they will hand you over to the local councils and flog you in their synagogues" (v. 17). "Brother will betray brother to death ... All men will hate you because of me" (vv. 21–22).

As His disciples are listening, no doubt more than a little confused, Jesus ties it all together. "Do not suppose that I have come to bring peace to the earth," He explains. "I did not come to bring peace, but a sword" (v. 34).

There they have it. That is their problem. They have thought, they have supposed, that Jesus is here to bring peace. They've assumed that this is the final chapter, that it's all over now, that the credits are rolling, and they will be riding into town as heroes with the crowds cheering and maybe even a little victory music playing in the background.

Jesus knows what they are thinking, and He wants to be perfectly clear with them right from the start. He states unambiguously, before they ever set foot out of camp, that He (and therefore they) is not bringing peace, but a sword.

Thirty-Six Inches

Now a sword is an interesting weapon. In our modern day, when we talk about warfare, we discuss snipers with an effective range of up to fifteen hundred feet, or cruise missiles with a range of fifteen hundred miles. But a sword? Well a sword has an effective range of about thirty-six inches. Used in intimate, hand-to-hand combat, a sword demands that its wielder step into the heart of mayhem. It places the warrior in an atmosphere of grave danger and offers no escape except to engage the enemy. What's more, winning a skirmish does little more than free the combatant up to fight another foe.

The picture was clear. The world was at war, and Peter and the rest of the disciples were going to be primary targets.

Nothing has really changed in the last two thousand years. With a wisdom that only comes from many years of swinging the kind of sword Jesus had in mind, Peter speaks to us today: "Dear friends, do not be surprised at the painful trial you are suffering, as though something strange were happening to you" (1 Peter 4:12). Yet we *are* surprised, aren't we? Like Jason Bourne, we seem to have forgotten that we're in the thick of a war.

Make no mistake: the world that you live in is at war. I don't care if you live in a mansion in Hollywood or on the streets of New York City, you are caught up in an epic battle. And it is not a battle in a far-away land; it takes place just thirty-six inches from your next step. Ignoring or minimizing this reality makes it no less true, any more than Jason Bourne's amnesia made him less of a target. Our enemy has not forgotten. He is, however, more than happy to keep us in the dark.

THE HEROIC PATH

Battle Ship or Cruise Liner

As Paul is warning the Christians in Corinth about false apostles, he explains that "Satan himself masquerades as an angel of light" (2 Corinthians 11:14). Satan has no desire to be seen as an enemy; he would much rather be recognized as the voice of reason. "Come on, now! All that religious hocus-pocus—you don't really believe it, do you? Life just happens, and you need to play the cards that it deals you. The important thing is that you are happy with you."

And if you're *not* happy with you?

"Well, just find something else that fulfills you."

My friend Gary Barkalow likens this mindset to being on a cruise liner rather than a battleship. On a cruise liner, if the food isn't fresh, the room clean, or the seas smooth, we complain to the captain. But on a battleship, food can wait until the bombing ends, and sailing on rough seas is much better than sinking in quiet waters.

The Bible repeatedly reminds us that we are not on a cruise ship, at least not now. Someday, yes, but right now we are in the greatest of battles. Listen to Paul speaking about his own inner life:

> I do not understand what I do. For what I want to do I do not do, but what I hate to do … As it is, it is no longer I myself who do it, but it is sin living in me. I know that nothing good lives in me, that is, in my sinful nature. For I have the desire to do what is good, but I cannot carry it out. For what I do is not the good I want to do; no, the evil I do not want to do—this I keep doing. Now if I do what I do not want to do, it is no longer I who do it, but it is sin living in me that does it. So I find this law at work: When I

want to do good, evil is right there with me. For in my inner being I delight in God's law; but I see another law at work in the members of my body, *waging war against the law of my mind and making me a prisoner to the law of sin at work within my members* (Romans 7:15,17–23, emphasis mine).

And that's just Paul describing his own struggles. Throughout his letters, you can also see his concern for the embattled churches under his care. For instance, Paul warns the Galatian believers that something has bewitched them (Galatians 3:1), deceiving and turning them from the faith that they have known. It doesn't take much of an imagination to realize who is at the heart of that bewitching.

Jesus teaches that He, the Good Shepherd, comes in through the gate. But there is a thief who also wants in. He doesn't come in announced through the front door. Instead, he climbs over the fence, tunnels under, or parachutes in. In other words, he gets in any way he can. His purpose? "The thief comes only to steal and kill and destroy" (John 10:10).

Slavery

If we have any hope of overcoming our personal wounds and failures, of stepping onto the heroic path and reengaging the life that Christ would have for us, we must understand something: When Jesus declared that He had come to set the captives free, it was us whom He was speaking of. We are the captives. Evil has invaded our land, our homes, and our lives, but we have unfortunately grown so accustomed to it that we have forgotten about it. Like refugees in a concentration camp, we have come to accept our condition as the only reality. We were born as slaves, we've grown up as slaves, we live in a world of slaves, and slavery is all we really know. Even when we are "born again," coming to know Christ and accepting His sacrifice for our salvation, this slavery mentality can still be almost impossible to escape.

This is because we are caught in a battle that our enemy, the Devil, fights on three primary fronts. The first is total darkness, as he attempts to keep us from knowing the love that Jesus has for us and the Life He offers.

Once we give our lives to Jesus, the battle doesn't end. Satan's second front is to convince us that all is good now. He reminds us that we are going to heaven some day, so we have little to worry about. "Go to church, pay your tithe, and keep quiet," is the message many of us understand as the Christian faith. We recognize that certain others are called to more, but we are just your average Joes, and our role has little to do with advancing the kingdom or fighting any battles.

And if we do dare to step out? We almost always encounter our enemy's third wave: frontal attack. Opposition materializes from seemingly nowhere. Our efforts seem futile. Our plans fail. Others may tell us that we don't have what it takes. So we concede. Back in our self-made bunker we find safety, a familiarity that at least offers some solitude and rest.

I hope you are starting to see the bigger picture here. Satan wants you to accept your defeats as proof that you should never have walked this road in the first place.

In a scene about halfway through *The Bourne Identity*, Jason begins to recognize the danger he is in and contacts his pursuers. They try to convince him that he is the problem and they are there to help him. They invite him to turn himself in; they promise to help him and end the madness. The truth, of course, is that they plan to kill him.

Sound familiar? Satan offers us a similar "truce." He presents it by challenging the truth as he did with Eve. "Did God really say …?" (Genesis 3:1). He's called the Deceiver for a reason. And the result is the same for Jason, for Eve, and for us: death.

The Truth

You are in a battle. As much as you don't want to believe it and as much as the world may tell you otherwise, it is the truth. All hell is set against you. Could there really be any other explanation? Just look back on your life. When has the battle been the fiercest? Hasn't it been during the times when you've tried to right a wrong or pursue something noble and great? Why else do so many marriages that start with genuine love and admiration end in bitter divorces? Why do so many deeply committed leaders find themselves caught in compromise and failure? Do you really believe that all of them were just bad people from the beginning?

A number of years ago, I began a journey. After years of walking with Christ and immersing myself in ministry, I was feeling the effects of wound after wound. Like Jason, I had no idea why. I seemed to be fighting the air, swinging wildly at nothing. Finally,

THE HEROIC PATH

after a deep moral failure, I was ready to just give it all up. Why try any longer?

Yet God, out of His grace, continued to pursue me and bring others into my life to offer counsel and wisdom. Through the Scriptures and a few good books, I began to recognize the pattern of our enemy's attacks and his reason behind them. He wanted to keep me quiet.

I began meeting with some men in my basement to discuss this battle, and one after another they, like me, found freedom and life. Jesus in His kindness began speaking to me in some deep and personal ways. He affirmed time and again through words, the Bible, and circumstances that equipping men to fight was my life's calling. So it was that Knight Vision Ministries was formed.

Our team began doing conferences, and I published my first book. We produced a number of teaching resources. We could sense God moving among us, and I had no doubt that I was discovering my own heroic path. I began to understand in a much deeper way the necessity and power of prayer.

Yet success was anything but sure. While many were touched by our ministry and my book, book sales and conference registrations certainly didn't break any records. Individuals who had committed to helping and supporting us experienced personal crises, which caused them to back away. Some people were openly critical of our efforts. And my personal life also presented more than a few issues and distractions. Apathy began to circle my heart like a vulture waiting for the carcass to stop moving.

Doubt has a way of replacing faith during such times. Certain as I had been of God's call on me, now I began to question it.

Maybe it was futile after all, no more than a pipe dream I had created in a subconscious attempt to find significance for my miserable life. God had never spoken, or if He had, I obviously had misunderstood Him. I was lost in a desert with no water and no sign of relief from the scorching sun.

Pursuing God and His plan for our lives does not protect us from the Enemy's barrages. Rather, it intensifies them. The attacks become personal, playing on our greatest fears and manipulating our smallest idiosyncrasies until we become disoriented, confused, and amnesiac of the truth we once knew clearly.

And merely being aware of the battle doesn't protect us. Yes, we need to know that we have an enemy, and we need to know that we are a target; that is a good place to start. But it isn't enough. Adam walked intimately with God in the garden in the most perfect of all relationships, yet still Adam fell. So great is the battle, so strong and resourceful is our enemy that mere awareness of his activity will never save us. We need more, much more. We need to know why our adversary wants to destroy us. Why us? Why now? Who are we that he would target us?

We need to begin restoring our memories. We need to find ourselves again.

TRAIL MARKERS

1. What are some of the "bad luck" experiences you have had as you've tried to do the right or noble thing?
2. What kinds of opposition have you experienced recently?
3. How do you tend to interpret life—as a cruise ship or a battleship? How do those around you interpret it?
4. Which of the fronts do you find yourself fighting on the most: the first, wondering if Jesus is even real; the second, wanting to just hang on until He returns; or the third, being actively opposed as you pursue His call on your life?
5. Look back at your walk with Christ up until today. Pay special attention to the times when you were trying to follow Jesus the closest. What were your circumstances? In what ways were you opposed in your pursuit of Jesus and His call on you? Do you believe the difficulties you encountered were just chance, or were they somehow orchestrated?
6. What effect did the opposition you experienced have on you?

Chapter Seven

Jesus's Call

Jesus calls us! O'er the tumult
Of our life's wild, restless sea.

Cecil Frances Alexander (1823–1895)

God authorized and commanded me to commission you:
Go out and train everyone you meet,
far and near, in this way of life …

Matthew 28:18–19 (The Message)

THE HEROIC PATH

It must have been an incredibly hard life: long nights, backbreaking labor, uncertain income, always at the mercy of the weather and lady luck. Yet, it also offered the rewards that drive men: close friendships, the thrill of the big score, and an existence solely dependent on one's skills and abilities. No bosses, no deadlines, just the need to pull up the old boot straps and dig a little deeper until success was yours. It was the ultimate man's job. It was fishing in the Lake of Gennesaret, better known as the Sea of Galilee, and Peter had done it all of his life.

In fact, that sea was his life, and Peter knew it well. It was the source of his livelihood, the cause of his greatest frustrations, and the foundation of the only victories that he had ever known. To call Peter a fisherman would have been akin to calling Bill Gates just another computer geek. There are many fishermen in the world, but Peter, he was a professional. His family survived on his skills. The Sea of Galilee was his home; his house was only a place to catch a bit of a rest between those grueling days on the boat.

That is largely what makes Peter's encounter with Jesus so intriguing. The gospel writer Luke records that Jesus was standing by the Lake of Gennesaret—Peter's lake—preaching to a crowd (Luke 5). Peter was at the lakeshore too, but he hadn't come to listen. He was doing what he did every morning: repairing nets after a long night's work. Once that task was accomplished, he would go home, catch a little shut-eye, and then return that evening for another shift.

Yet, he couldn't help but notice the multitudes or listen to the words of this man Jesus—how He captured the people's attention and spoke of a life that, no doubt, sounded foreign and a bit lofty to a man who had spent his life working with his hands and smelling like a bait shop. Peter must have felt both curious and a bit irritated. He just wanted to go home, but still something was echoing with his spirit, with his soul, with that part of him that had been longing for life.

Then, unexpectedly, Jesus commandeered one of Peter's boats in an attempt to place a few feet between Himself and the masses. Peter didn't object. Perhaps he even laid down his nets for a few minutes to listen to this strangely captivating man. He never anticipated what followed. Without warning, Jesus turned and looked directly at Peter. "Put out into deep water, and let down the nets for a catch."

"You have got to be kidding," Peter no doubt thought. "We've just finished repairing the nets for tonight. We are exhausted. And no offense, but I'm the expert here. There are no fish to be had today." But something Jesus had said, or something in His eyes, or perhaps just the peer pressure of the crowd caused Peter to consent.

You know the rest of the story. Fish! Fish so numerous that they threatened to swamp the small fishing boats. Peter may have been a man of simple means, but he was no idiot. He knew the sea, and he knew a mighty act of God when he saw one. "Go away from me Lord; I am a sinful man!"

Jesus wasn't performing parlor tricks to scare Peter, though. He was inviting him into a greater adventure, one that would take all of the brawn and determination of a full-time fisherman: He was calling Peter to follow Him. Peter did. And his life was never the same.

But it wasn't just Peter whom Jesus called. There were eleven others, and following them, the seventy, and the one hundred twenty. Later came Paul and Stephen and Barnabas and Timothy. If there is one consistency in how Jesus carries on His ministry and mission, it is in the way He calls men. Throughout the ages, in times of darkness and times of greatness, among both the wealthy and the outcasts, the haves and the have-nots, Jesus has continued to search for men who will answer His call. "For the eyes of the Lord range throughout the earth to strengthen those whose hearts are fully committed to him" (2 Chronicles 16:9). He's looking, He's searching—for you.

Marching Orders

Perhaps nothing else will transform your life in Christ more than this truth: you are called by God. Why, after experiencing horrifying circumstances, did the men who fought World War II return home and become a productive, successful generation while so many veterans of the Vietnam era struggle to this day? At least a part of the answer lies in the sense of calling these men had to their cause. World War II was embraced as the noble effort of brave men to free the world from tyranny. Vietnam, by contrast, was seen as an unnecessary and even evil war. Sadly, those returning did not receive the heroes' welcomes they deserved; instead, they were derided. The fault was not theirs. But they'd had no noble cause to fight for, no transcendent calling, and men need that type of mission in their lives. We were created for it.

Jesus's Call

"Fill the earth and subdue it. Rule over the fish of the sea and the birds of the air and over every living creature that moves on the ground" (Genesis 1:28). Those were our marching orders issued at our creation. We were put here to influence the world that we live in under a God-ordained anointing to accomplish His goals and dreams for this planet. And if God created us for that purpose, does it not make sense that He would instill in us a need, a desire, to fulfill it? Wouldn't a man, created to make a difference in the world, be forever frustrated until he began living out that calling?

So most of us men spend our lives searching for our calling. We may not realize that this is what we are doing. We may think we are simply looking for the next big deal, the next moment of glory, or maybe even just a hot one-night stand. But what we really are looking for is something that tells us we are making a mark. Influencing something. "Filling the earth and subduing it."

And, my friend, heroic impact is exactly what Jesus came to offer. Consider His words: "I have come that they may have life, and have it to the full." (John 10:10). "He has sent me to proclaim freedom for the prisoners and recovery of sight for the blind, to release the oppressed, to proclaim the year of the Lord's favor" (Luke 4:18–19). And so, "you will be my witnesses in Jerusalem, and in all Judea and Samaria, and to the ends of the earth" (Acts 1:8). To that end, "My prayer is not that you take them out of the world but that you protect them from the evil one. They are not of the world, even as I am not of it. Sanctify them by the truth; your word is truth. As you sent me into the world, I have sent them into the world" (John 17:15–18).

THE HEROIC PATH

Do you see it? The Gospel, in its simplest and purest form is this: Jesus came to set us free from our lives of futility and striving so that we could accomplish the thing He created us for from the beginning—to live lives of significance and great adventure as we stand side by side with our King ushering in His kingdom.

The Few and the Proud

That adventure, like all great quests, comes with a cost. How it must sadden our Father to see how we have cheapened His call. In our pursuit of walking in humility and reliance on all that He has done, we have forgotten that life in Christ also takes all that we are. Not that we add to the price Jesus paid for us, or that we in some way earn our salvation. No, redemption was accomplished only by Jesus and is available only in Him. However, Satan has managed to convince much of the church that our part is now simply one of waiting for Jesus to return. And while we wait, well, a few hymns and a weekly sermon can't hurt.

Jesus, however, keeps stirring the pot, saying things like, "The kingdom of heaven has been forcefully advancing, and forceful men lay hold of it" (Matthew 11:12) and, "If anyone would come after me, he must deny himself and take up his cross daily and follow me" (Luke 9:23). To one potential disciple who wanted first to bury his father, Jesus said, "Let the dead bury their own dead, but you go and proclaim the kingdom of God" (Luke 9:60) and to another who simply wanted to say goodbye to his family,

Jesus's Call

Jesus replied, "No one who puts his hand to the plow and looks back is fit for service in the kingdom of God" (Luke 9:62).

Is Jesus really that cruel and insensitive? Of course not. We see His heart and His compassion in every aspect of His life. So what is the deal with these demands? They can only be understood in the context of a greater story and with the realization of a great need.

If all that Jesus has for us on this side of eternity is to stand around a campfire singing "Kumbaya," then yes, His demands are tactless at the least, and even evil and destructive. But what if Jesus knew something that we did not? What if the kingdom of heaven really was meeting resistance, and what if the only way it could advance and achieve a true, lasting peace were for us to take our places on the front lines? What if the survival of the human race, the survival of your wife and children, were dependant on your participation in this kingdom and its battles?

On September 11, 2001, the United States was attacked by terrorists. Most of us remember exactly what we were doing that morning as the images of the burning and then collapsing twin towers in New York City streamed across our televisions and computer screens. What followed was perhaps even more significant. Men and women, many of which had been apathetic and lethargic in regard to any kind of patriotism, suddenly began flooding the Army recruiting offices. The true heart of America was revealed to be alive and willing to risk whatever it took to stop this evil. Al Qaeda's attempt to destroy our nation had actually brought it together.

So it is with Jesus's call. As we have already pointed out, we are in a battle. The casualties have been real. We have, every one of us, been wounded and shot down on some level. And in that context, Jesus's words are not so extreme. They are rather the words of a wise friend inviting us to step into the story and be counted among the few and the proud.

Sons of the King

A few years ago my family rented a movie titled *In the Name of the King: A Dungeon Siege Tale* starring Jason Statham. It is the story of a man known only by the name Farmer. He is living a life that many men would admire, married to a beautiful woman, raising a handsome young son, and working the land with his hands. He has all that he could ever want. With no great dreams of power or riches, Farmer is content with the simple and the peaceful.

As with all great stories, though, nothing is truly as it seems. Farmer's peaceful existence is illusory; the land is at war with an evil, supernatural being known as the Krug. It attacks the village where Farmer lives, kills his young son, and takes his wife captive. The king of the land seeks men from the village to raise an army to fight this evil. But Farmer, angry with the kingdom for not protecting his family and wounded by his own loss, turns his back on his king.

Trying desperately to recreate his perfect little world, the peaceful box that he had fashioned for his own comfort and enjoyment, Farmer is confronted by the king's personal magus, who asks Farmer a revealing question: "Has it occurred to you that there may be events of greater importance than the loves and losses of our particular lives?"

Jesus's Call

Farmer looks the old sage in the eyes. "No, it hasn't occurred to me," he says, and walks away.

But you see, what Farmer doesn't know yet is that he is the long-lost son of the king. He alone has royal blood flowing through him. And only that blood has the power to destroy the evil that has taken over the land. Until Farmer recognizes this truth and embraces his destiny, he has no hope of restoring any true peace in his life.

As I watched the movie, I was stunned, for it is *our* story. We, too, tend to live lives that are smaller than we really are, creating our safe little boxes of comfort and peace. But sooner or later, evil attacks our safe places, leaving us confused, hurt, disoriented, and struggling to find some way to put what we once had back together again. As with Farmer, our King has called us to step into a larger story, an event of greater importance than the loves and losses of our particular lives. But, like Farmer, the pain of our wounds has blinded us to that truth and maybe even embittered us to it. We are determined to make things work out on our own, to take matters into our own hands. For we too have forgotten.

Listen to one of our own sages, whose name is Paul. "You did not receive a spirit that makes you a slave again to fear, but you received the Spirit of sonship. And by him we cry, '*Abba*, Father.' The Spirit himself testifies with our spirit that we are God's children. Now if we are children, then we are heirs—heirs of God and co-heirs with Christ" (Romans 8:15–17).

The truth is, we are sons of the King, invited to His table, adopted as His heirs. And it is to us that He, our King, has entrusted His kingdom. That safe little world we thought we were building—it was never safe, and it was never the friend we thought it was. *It* has been our enemy. "If you belonged to the world, it would love you as its own. As it is, you do not belong to the world, but I have chosen you out of the world. That is why the world hates you" (John 15:19).

Jesus has chosen you; He has called you. Your salvation was free, but it was also an invitation to walk into a life of transcendence, a life you were created to live in.

Following Peter's confession that Jesus was the Christ, the Son of the living God, Jesus made a powerful statement. I believe He was speaking not only to Peter, but to all of us. Listen: "On this rock [this confession] I will build my church, and the gates of Hades will not overcome it. I will give you the keys of the kingdom of heaven; whatever you bind on earth will be bound in heaven, and whatever you loose on earth will be loosed in heaven" (Matthew 16:18–19). Jesus was, and is, offering us the keys to the castle. He has left it in our hands.

Jesus is coming back soon. "However, when the Son of Man comes, will he find faith on the earth?" (Luke 18:8). Wasn't that, after all, the point of Jesus's parable of the talents? You remember the story in Matthew, chapter twenty-five. A man goes on a journey, leaving his property entrusted to his men. "After a long time," the narrative reads, "the master of those servants returned." For the first two servants, the rewards were great. Then came the third guy, who had taken what the master entrusted to him and hid it. "His master replied, 'You wicked, lazy servant!'" Ouch!

Jesus's Call

Those are some pretty harsh words for a man who really didn't squander anything and at worse just misunderstood the heart of his master—unless, again, we recognize that we are in a war for our very lives. Unless we understand that much more is at stake than we realize. Then the question becomes pertinent: "When the Son of Man comes, will he find faith?" Like an army commander who understands that all are at risk when one doesn't take his place in the operation, so this master also understands the enormity of each man's role in his kingdom.

That kingdom is the kingdom of heaven, and you are one of the servants to whom it has been entrusted. Your significance in this kingdom is more than you can imagine. What your role is and why it is so important will be our next focus. Just know this: Jesus is looking you in the eyes and urging you to head out once again into the deep water and put down your nets.

TRAIL MARKERS

1. In what ways have you felt frustrated because your life is not all it was made to be? How have you attempted to fill the void?
2. How might it change your life if you knew that the survival of your family and your world were hanging in the balance, and you were called to affect that balance?
3. "Has it occurred to you that there may be events of greater importance than the loves and losses of our particular lives?" Elaborate on your thoughts.
4. Is it possible that the life you're living is smaller than you really are and less than it was meant to be?
5. What do you believe is Jesus's call on your life right now, and how do you feel about it? Do you doubt it, accept it, fear it, hope it is true, or wish it were not?

Chapter Eight

Why Me?

There is no passion to be found playing small—in settling for a life that is less than the one you are capable of living.

Nelson Mandela

For God did not give us a spirit of timidity, but a spirit of power, of love and of self-discipline.

2 Timothy 1:7

THE HEROIC PATH

CNN called him "The Man in the Red Bandanna." Twenty-four-year-old Welles Crowther had always dreamed of being a firefighter or maybe even a CIA agent, but the necessities of life had left him working behind a desk as an equities trader. He excelled; yet he told his dad that he wished he were in the field rather than in an office so he could actively help others.

Welles did his job well, always friendly, unassuming, another face in the massive mosaic of corporate America. Perhaps his only real defining mark was the red bandana he always carried in his back pocket, a habit he had picked up from his father.

That all changed in the early morning hours of September 11, 2001, as Crowther sat at his desk on the 104th floor of the South Tower in the World Trade Center. After the first plane struck the North Tower, Crowther called his mother to assure her that he was okay. He then apparently began making his way down the stairwell despite announcements that building occupants should stay put. That's when the second plane hit.

Ling Young was waiting by an express elevator on the seventy-eighth floor when the second United jet slammed into that same floor and burst into flame. Ling was left bloodied and dazed; most of those around her were dead.

Suddenly Welles Crowther stepped through a door sporting a red bandana over his mouth. In a calm and commanding voice, he began ushering the survivors to an exit and down the stairwell. After assisting the severely burned Ling to safety and carrying another young woman on his back, the young desk-jockey began making his way back up the stairwell to help others. With his clear, directive voice, Crowther continued to lead many more to safety right up to the moment when the South Tower could stand no longer.

Welles Crowther's body wasn't recovered until March 2002. He was found, unburned, in the lobby of the South Tower alongside rescue workers and firefighters who had been running a command center during one of America's soberest moments in history.

What is it that causes a bright, successful twenty-four-year-old man to choose not to save himself, but instead, to sacrifice his future and his potential in order to deliver those around him safely out of the chaos? What is it that produces a hero out of a boy and invites him into something transcendent and holy?

Part of the answer, I believe, lies in the relationship that Welles Crowther had with his dad. Working in his teen years with his father, a volunteer firefighter, Welles clearly received a sense of identity and self-sacrifice—a transfer from father to son. Welles knew in a way that cannot be taught, only absorbed in the presence of another, that how he lived every moment of his life mattered.

Glory amid the Stones

Stephen was another man who understood the importance of each moment. Since he grew up amid first-century Jewish culture, we can only speculate about his early life. He likely at least knew who Jesus was during His time on earth; however, it wasn't until after Christ's ascension that this young man, Stephen, appears on the radar screen.

THE HEROIC PATH

In Acts, chapter six, we are told that a dispute had broken out among the early believers. It seems that some of the widows were being ignored in the daily distribution of food. Peter and the other eleven apostles—the front men if you will—recognized that this was a serious concern; however their duties as leaders afforded them no time to address the issue. So, wisely, they appointed a committee of seven men to resolve the conflict.

Stephen was one of the men chosen. Right from the start we notice something strong and magnificent about this man. Acts 6:5 tells us he was "full of faith and of the Holy Spirit." He had an air about him that said all was well, even when all was anything but well. It was faith and it was God. Yet despite his inner strength, or perhaps because of it, Stephen was honored to "wait on tables." Gary Barkalow would call this Stephen's assignment. It wasn't Stephen's calling to serve the widows, but it was a place, during this time, where his strength as a man combined with his calling as a son of the King in such a way that the glory of his life was evident.

Maybe too evident. Not only were lives being touched locally by Stephen, but apparently the entire old order was being shaken by this man and others like him. Rather than splintering and dissolving as many Jewish leaders believed would happen, the church was growing. Inspired no doubt by the quiet strength of men such as Stephen, many were joining this new movement of Christ-followers, much to the dismay of the more militantly religious sects of the day. That's when the tower began to fall.

Called out, questioned, and accused by the early church's terrorist opposers, Stephen had only moments to act. And boy, did he. Preaching the sermon of a lifetime, Stephen made clear the path to life. Then he died, crushed by stones much like Welles Crowther—not in fear, but with the clearest vision of his life of what it was that God had placed him on earth to do.

Created in Greatness

Each of us men has a similar glory, a strength to our lives akin to that of Stephen and Welles. It may not always be evident, but it is there. It was placed there by our Creator.

As God created this universe, repeatedly He looked it over and declared it good. Of course it was. Just look at the world around you: trees, mountains, thunderstorms, butterflies, creatures living in the depths of the sea that no man has yet seen, solar systems that we may never see … creation was magnificent, engineered by God Himself. Then God created man in His own image, and of His new masterpiece God said, "*very* good." Despite our flaws and failures, we are, at our deepest core, the crown jewel of God's creation. Not just good, not just magnificent, but very good.

And if you think that the fall destroyed that, think again. The entire Bible after the second chapter of Genesis is the story of God pursuing us, His prized creation. He spares no expense, until finally He gives His very life for us. It is the ultimate story of rescue. You don't see God giving Himself for stars that are dying or polar ice caps that are melting; but for us, for man, He literally changes history.

That, my friend, is because of who you are.

THE HEROIC PATH

I've heard many preachers preach and worship leaders sing about how it's all about God, not us. I agree: it is all about Him. He is, after all, God. It is His name that will be made great among the nations, and it is to Him that every knee will bow. He alone deserves worship and glory and honor, and none can ever compare to Him.

However, I also disagree. It is really all about us. All the battles of the Bible, all the rescues from the enemy, the "restoration of all things" that Jesus came to accomplish—all of it has but one purpose: to restore us, God's creation, to the place for which He formed us. It is the ultimate compliment, the greatest love story ever told. God laid aside His peace and comfort to redeem us. He could have just wiped the slate clean and started over. He could have forced His will on us and demanded our worship. Instead, He woos us as only a lover would do. God doesn't demand; He invites. Because He needs us? No, God doesn't need anything. But He *wants* us. He values and desires us. He values and desires *you*.

And that makes you a prime target for the Enemy.

Jealous Hatred

Painting a picture of a time long before ours, the prophet Ezekiel addresses a certain personage with these words: "You were the model of perfection, full of wisdom and perfect in beauty. You were in Eden, the garden of God; every precious stone adorned you … Your settings and mountings were made of gold … You were anointed as a guardian cherub" (Ezekiel 28:12–14). Most scholars agree that while this passage is spoken to the king of Tyre, it is in truth a reference to the source of the king's corruption, Satan.

Eons ago, before our chapter in the story ever began, our enemy was the apple of our King's eyes. But Satan wanted more. Longing for God's glory not just His love, Satan began longing for power until finally he could stand it no more. Revelation 12:7–9 gives us a glimpse into that fateful day:

> And there was war in heaven. Michael and his angels fought against the dragon, and the dragon and his angels fought back. But he was not strong enough, and they lost their place in heaven. The great dragon was hurled down—that ancient serpent called the devil, or Satan, who leads the whole world astray. He was hurled to the earth, and his angels with him.

That is where we find Satan at the beginning of our story: in the Garden. How he must have hated us, created in the image of God with all of those god-like traits: creativity, jurisdiction, free will, and worst of all, the adoration of God Himself. It's no wonder that the Serpent attacked Adam with such vengeance, driving him from the very presence of God.

But as you know, his plan didn't work. God didn't abandon mankind; rather, He pursued us. That pursuit culminated on Calvary, where the Creator of the universe demonstrated conclusively that the words of Solomon were really the words of God concerning us: "I am my beloved's and my beloved is mine" (Song of Songs 6:3 KJV).

THE HEROIC PATH

Mystery

Much of the apostle Paul's writing focuses on conveying the full extent of God's heart for us in this mystery we call the Gospel. With good reason too. I doubt that we could ever imagine such a grand tale, let alone convince ourselves it were true, if it hadn't been written down by such a powerful man of God.

During the last few weeks, I've found myself caught up in a television series. It's one of those prime time soap operas where you kind of know what's going on, but not really. An alien race has invaded earth, but I'm not sure whether they are the good guys or the bad guys, or what their true intentions are. Not knowing is driving me crazy! I hate waiting each week for a small morsel of information only to be left with more questions than answers.

In Colossians 1:26–27, Paul explains that God had written a similar mystery and kept it concealed far longer than any fall television series. But at last, says Paul, "the mystery that has been hidden for ages and generations … is now disclosed to the saints." No more waiting, no more tuning in next week to find out. Now, Paul says, we know the secret. And boy, is it a shocker! No one would have guessed. "This mystery … is Christ in you."

Now imagine how Satan, who aspired to the place of God, feels about Him taking up residence in you. I mean, really—*you?* The one whom the Devil so easily manipulated into eating the apple? The one he has used to make war on God's creation, to pollute the world, to laugh at human rights? This vile and fallen creature, this failure of creation, is the one in whom God has chosen to dwell?

It's absurd and it makes no sense. The act proclaims clearly to Satan and the entire universe, even if we miss it, that we, mankind, hold a very special place in the heart of God.

It's no surprise, then, that destroying the life Christ created and redeemed us for has become the primary work of Satan. As Paul further explains, we are sons of God and co-heirs with Christ (Romans 8:14-17) and that God's love for us is like that of a groom for his bride (Ephesians 5:25-32), we can begin to understand the hatred that wells up in this fallen angel.

Satan sees you as possessing all that he ever wanted. It is you who will rule with Christ, you for whom Jesus is preparing a dwelling place, and you whom He has pursued all of these years. So you see, in a way, it really is all about you.

Lies, Lies, Lies

Satan's strategy is to convince us otherwise: that we are merely byproducts of our environment, or at best the afterthoughts of a busy and uninterested deity. Thus we spend our days living small, never aspiring to true greatness. We deny the work of Christ and in its place settle for lives of never rocking the boat. Lives of conformity, and ultimately, of impotence.

Do you see it? Have you observed the results of our enemy's unrelenting assault on our identity? He has effectively immobilized the armies of God. Just look at our churches. So much effort is expended just to keep the congregations interested and engaged. Church growth books talk about the back-door effect, with a steady flow of members leaving one church in search of another. It's not that the people are bad or even the churches are bad. However, our enemy has convinced us that our only viable role is that of happy and committed members of an organization.

Once the contentment our role promised us wears thin, the only answer is to move on.

But remember, Satan is a liar, the father of all lies. Lying is what he does. Is it any wonder, then, that in preparing believers for battle, Paul first instructs us to put on the belt of truth (Ephesians 6:14). The belt Paul had in mind was the part of a Roman soldier's armor that held everything else together. The sword in its scabbard hung from the belt. The belt kept everything else in its place for the soldier.

Our belt is truth. Until we grasp the truth, we will forever be the victims of lies.

What Is Truth?

It's no accident that Paul uses the analogy of the belt of truth at the end of Ephesians; much of the first half of his letter concerns our identity in Christ. Paul tells us that we were chosen in Christ,[5] predestined to be adopted as God's sons, marked in Christ with the seal of the Holy Spirit, and made alive in Him. It gets even better. We have been raised with Christ and seated in the heavenly realms with Him, and now we are members of God's household.

---

5 Scripture references for this and the rest of Paul's statements are, in order, Ephesians 1:4, 5, 13; and 2:5, 6, 19.

Why Me?

"As a prisoner for the Lord, then," Paul continues, "I urge you to live a life worthy of the calling you have received" (Ephesians 4:1).

Paul was saying, in no uncertain terms, that there is something magnificent about your life. You have been redeemed for greatness—not because of any meritorious action on your part, but as a result of the relentlessness with which the God of the universe has pursued you.

That is why your life has been opposed at every step. That is why you are a target in the battle. It is because you are a prince, a son of the King. You are the object of God's affection, and Satan absolutely hates that fact. More, he fears it because once you arm yourself with the belt of truth and take your rightful place in God's kingdom, then Satan's lies become exposed for what they really are. You fight and win in this unseen war by confronting lies with truth. Isn't that how Jesus did it? When Satan tempted Him in the desert, He met each attack with a word of truth.

Why me? Why you? Because your strength is needed. Because, like it or not, war is upon us and your time to rise up and assume your part will come. One word of warning: don't let the Enemy lie to you, convincing you that your time already came and went, and the building fell without you stepping up. The fact that you are still upright and breathing is evidence of God's continued plan for you.

God chose you in Christ before the creation of the world. Where you are right now is not an afterthought, a Plan B. It has been God's plan all along that you should be here, at your desk on the 104th floor on this day in history. Satan knows this, which

THE HEROIC PATH

is why he has opposed you. God also knows it, which is why He has never stopped pursuing you. You are the only one who is uncertain. But that is okay; believing God even when you are uncertain is the essence of faith, isn't it.

Why you? Why not you? You are here at this time and in this place. It may not be where you thought you would be when all hell broke loose, and you honestly may be a bit surprised that a terrorist would choose your life to attack. But hey, check out your back pocket. I'll bet there's a bandana in there somewhere.

TRAIL MARKERS

1. It is all about God, yet it's also all about us: How do you feel about that statement? Does it strike you as heresy? Good news? Why?
2. Why would Satan pick a battle with you? What qualities has God imparted to humans that make us the object of the Devil's wrath?
3. Have you ever felt as if you were just an "afterthought of a very busy and uninterested Deity"? Who would gain the most from your thinking this way?
4. Read the first couple of chapters of the book of Ephesians. Who, what, and where does it say you are in and through Christ?
5. What do your answers to the previous question suggest about the significance of your life?

Chapter Nine

Orientation

I know it's hard, when you're up to your armpits in alligators, to remember you came here to drain the swamp.

Ronald Reagan

Dear friends, do not be surprised at the fiery ordeal that has come on you to test you, as though something strange were happening to you.

1 Peter 4:12 (NIV, 2011 edition)

THE HEROIC PATH

Six days—not even a week, yet an eternity. Six days. That's how long it took Aron Ralston to arrive at the conclusion that his only way down off of the mountain was to cut his own hand off.

In the spring of 2003 Aron, a young, independent, passionate mountaineer, was doing what he loved, what he lived for: rock climbing, canyoneering, and hiking in the mountains of Utah. Climbing was his life; it *gave* him life. But today, it appeared that climbing might also take his life.

While Aron was climbing alone in a remote area, a 1000-pound boulder had shifted and pinned his hand to the canyon wall. For six days, Aron had considered the situation. With the small video camera he had brought along to record his trip, he had even gone so far as to tape his last will and testament. The rock was immovable, and Aron was hungry, tired and dehydrated. Even as he considered the unthinkable—amputating his own hand to save his life—Aron realized that the small multi-tool he had brought with him would never cut through the heavy bones of his forearm.

That's when Aron had a revelation: he could use the boulder as a counter-lever and break the bones free. It would be a gruesome and unquestionably painful procedure. But it would also be life—almost like being raised from the dead, Aron would later report. And so, after six days of facing certain extinction, Aron Ralston cut off his own hand and began a seventeen-mile hike to his truck, where he was found by other hikers and airlifted to a hospital and into the ranks of legend.

Orientation

Aron Ralston has since finished solo climbing all fifty-three of Colorado's 14,000-foot peaks in the winter (reportedly the first person ever to do so). He has solo climbed the 20,000-foot peak of Denali, scaled Mt. Kilimanjaro, and plans to tackle Everest sometime soon. He has also become a regular motivational speaker, sharing his six days trapped in Blue John Canyon, as well as a husband and a father. Aron's philosophy: "A hand and a forearm are not life."

Neither is any other wound. Neither are your wounds. What you lost was not life. Oh, it may have felt like it, and the loss may have even drastically changed your life, but it was not life. You are still here. Your journey is not over, not yet.

I cannot imagine the psychological challenge that losing a hand represents to a mountain climber. To a runner, a hand is nice; to a race car driver, it is important; to a construction worker, it is very useful; but to a mountain climber—most climbers would consider it impossible to go on without one. Every move requires gripping, pinching, hanging, lunging. To not have a hand is to not be able to climb. At least, that's what everyone else would say.

But not Aron Ralston. To him, not having a hand has seemed to further define who he is, what his deepest drive and desires are. Rather than ending Aron's climbing, losing his hand inspired it. Aron has two separate prostheses with which he switches back and forth depending on the move he's about to make. If he had any doubt before, there is no question now that climbing is what his life is about.

THE HEROIC PATH

Misreading Messages

Our greatest losses tend to strike at the heart of our deepest desires. If I've set my sights on winning the hundred-yard-dash, then I may feel a broken toe much more acutely than a failed investment.

But there's more to our losses than disappointment and heartbreak alone. We have an enemy who fears us and what we may become. He knows something about each of us, something that perhaps we haven't yet grasped.

Drawing on thousands of years of experience, Satan recognizes in each of us our potential from a very young age. Much of the wounding you have experienced was orchestrated by him in a sinister plan to purge your God-given desires and gifts from your life.

Of course, some of your injuries were just bad luck, and some were actually God challenging and refining you. But others, especially the darkest and ugliest wounds, were strategically directed strikes against the very heart of what Christ has for you.

Allow me to share part of my story. I was born to an unwed thirty-something woman who already had four children. Unable to adequately care for her present children and embarrassed by her fall for a married man, she put me up for adoption.

By God's grace, I was placed in a loving Christian home. The adoption was never kept secret from me, but rather was touted as a reminder of how much my adoptive parents wanted me. It was a deep sense of pride to me.

Yet still there was a realization that someone else didn't want me. I don't think I ever really put words to it, but I see now how

I acted it out, wanting desperately to be identified as part of my adoptive family. I went to extreme lengths to prove that I was just like the others in my new family. I wanted desperately to be identified as a Kortje man.

Then, as I grew, I developed a speech impediment. With years of speech therapy, my enunciation improved; still, especially when I was tired, I could be hard to understand.

One day, at the impressionable age of sixteen, when a boy is trying to fit into a man's world, I was sitting at a breakfast table with my best friend and his stepfather, a wounded, angry alcoholic who blamed the world for his failures. The stepfather asked me a question, and whatever I said in reply, it came out mumbled. The man's response cut to my heart as a young boy: "God damn it, Kortje, you talk like you've got your mouth full of shit."

Pardon the expletives, but I want you to understand the sharpness of that statement. The message was clear to me: I had nothing to say, and whatever I did say would only lead to more shame.

A short while later, no doubt trying to snap me out of my downward spiral of teenage rebellion, a high school counselor told me that I would never amount to anything. Determined to prove him wrong (or perhaps right), I attended college and then medical school, largely in an attempt to find some identity.

It was while I was in medical school that I came to Christ, and I quickly found myself involved in Christian leadership. Unfortunately, ministry can bring out the deepest insecurities both in oneself and in others. Over the next few years, I experienced accusations and attacks by those I had thought were friends and abandonment by leaders I had loved and trusted. I'm not so naïve as to think that none of it was my own doing; I'm certain I brought much of it on myself. The issue isn't who was at fault, but what those experiences did to my heart.

Other circumstances also took their toll. Once, while delivering a sermon at the church I had helped start, I suddenly became confused and disoriented. I heard myself talking, but I knew that my words were not making a lot of sense. My listeners stared at me blankly from their pews, trying to look interested. I finished with a halfhearted "amen" and sat down. Again the message I got was clear: Each time you step out to speak and to share your glory, Kortje, you fail. You are not wanted. You have nothing that anyone needs.

This didn't happen every day, of course. I had many successes. But the failures occurred often enough that, over time, they left a deep wound in my heart. Did I really have any value, anything important to say?

Now here I am today, speaking at churches and events, leading a ministry to walk men through their battles, and sharing my thoughts with you in these pages. Yet even as I write, a voice in me is laughing, telling me my readers will conclude that I really do have nothing to say. Satan's voice of self-doubt is persistent. But it is not the truth, and it is not the only voice. Another, more powerful Voice calls me forward. That Voice is our King, who speaks better things of me, of you, of us all.

Orientation

Recognizing Patterns

Looking back at my life, at the wounds I have encountered, I see in them a pattern. They almost tell a story.

Many of our deepest wounds are aimed at our greatest glory, and they cause us to doubt that glory. Almost from birth, throughout our childhood and teen years, and even as grown men under the blood of Christ, a war has raged against our hearts to keep us from living the lives we were created to live. It is diabolical.

However, it is also revealing. If you examine your own life and consider when and how you received your wounds, more than likely you, like me, will discover a pattern. It may be sketchy at first, but stick with it. Look closely. Where were you put down or shut up? When did you fail miserably when you were so sure that you were right? What is it that you vowed never to try again? This is exactly where the Enemy wants to take you: to a place of making a vow, an agreement with him that some area of your life will be avoided at all costs.

Joseph must have had such thoughts. As a boy he had a dream. A couple of dreams actually, but they both said the same thing: one day his father and brothers would bow down to him. When he shared that dream with his family—well, all did not go as hoped. His brothers sold him to a group of traveling slave traders.

Yet even as a slave in Potiphar's home, Joseph's glory was evident. Perhaps, Joseph once again began to believe that he was made to be a leader—until, again, betrayal stripped him of any glory he might have gained. Alone in a dungeon in a foreign land, forgotten by his family, Joseph seemed to have little hope for his

# THE HEROIC PATH

miserable life. The words of the Enemy must have sounded crystal clear: "Your dream was a farce. You are nothing. Every time you try to exert your gifting, things get worse. Wake up and see the truth: you're just a poor, homeless shepherd. This prison is your home now. You might as well accept it."

I suspect that Aron Ralston heard similar voices: "Your hand is lost, and you can't climb without a hand. You will never climb again. This prison is your home now. You might as well accept it." The truth, though, was that the prison was not home—not Aron's home, not Joseph's home, and it doesn't have to be your home. Instead, it can be a guide, a clue to who you really are. Satan may have planned your destruction, but God is in the business of using our enemy's sinister plans for our good—in this case, our enlightenment.

Look back, way back. Sit down with a paper and pen and review your life, especially your wounds. Don't do it alone; ask Jesus to walk with you along the streets where you have walked, through the darkest allies and in the coldest nights. Write down what you see, what you remember. For instance, if there was abuse, how were you abused? What was your reaction to the abuse? What did it tell you about yourself, and what was your response to what it said? Did you agree with it? Did you make a vow, either verbally or in your heart, to never give yourself in that way again? Have you arranged your life so as to never again feel that kind of pain?

What you will likely discover is that there are consistencies in your wounds. Individually, they won't make a lot of sense. Just because your third-grade class laughed at you when you attempted to imitate Bon Jovi during the talent contest doesn't suggest that you weren't meant to be a rock star; it may just mean that you looked ridiculous. But you may also begin to see a pattern. Perhaps many times when you tried to "proclaim" something—when you got onstage or stood up in a crowd—you got shot down. If those were times when you were living in your desires, pay special attention. You may in fact have been discovering your place in the story; you just weren't fully prepared or trained. Satan loves to use such moments of failure to lead you to some awful conclusions about your life. Much like modern aversion therapy, which uses a negative stimulus such as electrical shock in order to break a habit, Satan uses shame, belittlement, and embarrassment to convince you that God never intended you to pursue the desires for which He Himself created you.

Sins or moral failures may also have tripped you up as you tried to pursue godly dreams. The scars from such occasions certainly don't amend the sin. They may, however, reveal the battle strategy that was used to distract you from your calling. In the midst of such devastation, you may have concluded, as many men do, that you are evil, corrupt, and unredeemable, and have no right to pretend to possess any form of godliness. But such self-loathing is not at all consistent with what the Scriptures say about who you are as a son of the living God. Just the opposite: It shows how intensely Satan is working to keep you from walking in your glory. And it's all the more reason why you need to fight back.

Signs: that's really what the mosaic of our lives can be if we take the time to look. M. Night Shyamalan's 2002 sci-fi blockbuster *Signs* weaves this concept throughout the film in the actions and lives of its characters. From Bo's obsession with leaving unfinished glasses of water around the home, and in so doing, eventually saving the family from an attacking alien, to Morgan's "curse" of asthma, which renders him incapable of inhaling a poison gas, the idea is that our lives are much more intricate and interrelated than we realize.

The question really comes down to whether our lives are just a series of random events with no rhyme or reason to them, or whether, as Mel Gibson's character concludes, there are no coincidences. Maybe the answer involves a bit of both. But if you follow the clues, the signs, you'll find that a picture—or more accurately, a map—often materializes, offering some much-needed orientation in this maze of life.

Like Aron Ralston, you can look at your crushed and deformed appendage and the hopelessness it has bred in your heart and realize that "a hand and a forearm are not life." More, you can begin to understand how they in fact point to the life you were meant to live.

The wounds of your life by no means tell the whole story of who you are; rather, they are clues, pieces of the puzzle. Now let's look ahead, not with the wisdom that comes from hindsight, but with revelation bestowed by a heavenly Father who wants you to see the big picture of what He has in store for you.

TRAIL MARKERS

1. Do the following exercise from the text: "Look back, way back. Sit down with a paper and pen and review your life, especially your wounds. Don't do it alone; ask Jesus to walk with you along the streets where you have walked, through the darkest allies and in the coldest nights. Write down what you see, what you remember. For instance, if there was abuse, how were you abused? What was your reaction to the abuse? What did it tell you about yourself, and what was your response to what it said? Did you agree with it? Did you make a vow, either verbally or in your heart, to never give yourself in that way again? Have you arranged your life so as to never again feel that kind of pain?"
2. Do you see any signs of Satan consistently trying to destroy something in you? How might God have been trying to mature that quality—or perhaps other qualities—at the same time?

Chapter Ten

For Your Eyes Only

*The trick to forgetting the big picture is
to look at everything close-up.*

Chuck Palahniuk

*For those God foreknew he also predestined
to be conformed to the likeness of his Son.*

Romans 8:29

THE HEROIC PATH

"Some things in life are just too hard to understand." I have probably said that to a thousand people in my life. It's usually in the context of a disturbing situation that I don't comprehend, but in which I want to offer some empathy in the midst of the confusion. Often the circumstances surround a loss of some type—a death, a failure, or maybe a deep personal attack.

Recently I shared those words with a friend on the verge of a divorce, struggling with why his wife would leave him after thirty-six years of marriage. My friend was in pain, shattered by the knowledge that his lifelong partner had chosen another man over him. There I sat with a person who was a man's man: strong, confident, outspoken, and bold, now sitting in my office, crying, broken, and asking that perennial question, "Why?"

"I don't know, Tom," I replied. "Some things in life are just too hard to understand."

I lied. I did understand. Maybe not all of the details, maybe not the specifics of why my friend was experiencing this devastation right now or why the timing of it might very well take him to the edge of no return. I honestly didn't understand all of the circumstances that led up to the separation: who was really at fault, what role Tom may have played, or what his wife's feelings might have been. I certainly didn't want to put some religious, judgmental spin on his emotions. But I did understand. Now just wasn't the time or place to walk my friend through all of that.

But I understood. Like all of us, Tom was on a journey, a path that was his alone. That path had three major players in it, and they were not, as he assumed, his wife, his pain, and "that guy she chose to shack up with." Of course, those three were real and significant, but they were not the chief players.

No, there was something much deeper happening here—the big picture, if you will. It involved the molding of Tom's character by God, the attack of his faith by Satan, and his personal choices regarding how he would interpret the situation.

Understand, I am not saying that God caused the affair, or even that the devil did, apart from his influence on the choices made by the various parties. What I am saying is that my friend was too close to the action to understand all that was happening around him. Once he, at some point, did begin to understand, he would be better equipped to respond to his crisis productively.

Character Molding

By now, you are no doubt beginning to recognize the cast in this great drama a bit more clearly yourself. Let's begin with God. What is He up to in the story of your own life? What is the big picture that He has for you? I'm not talking generalities such as making His name great or evangelizing the world. No doubt God's plan for you does involve those broader objectives; however, I am referring to the specific thesis that the Author of your life is weaving into your unique voyage. What is He up to with you, and how might He be using your current state of affairs to shape the future that was planned for you from the beginning?

Of course, only you can know the specifics, and in future chapters you'll find out how you can explore those aspects of your

THE HEROIC PATH

life that are uniquely yours. Right now, though, let's look at some foundational generalities. Understanding them is fundamental as you seek to interpret the chaos that presents itself daily.

Let's begin with the beginning: "Then God said, 'Let us make man in our image, in our likeness' ... So God created man in his own image, in the image of God he created him" (Gen 1: 26, 27). You were created in the image of God—a portrait of God, if you will, set in the midst of His creation.

But that image became the object of Satan's wrath, such that man fell. And what a fall it was! The marring and disfigurement of God's image in humankind is largely what set in motion the coming of our Savior to redeem us and restore us back to the original image of God. This restoration is what Paul had in mind when he wrote, "We all, who with unveiled faces contemplate the Lord's glory, are being transformed into his image with ever-increasing glory" (2 Corinthians 3:18 NIV, 2011 edition). In order to fully interpret the events of your life, you must begin here. God is in the process, through the work of His Holy Spirit, of molding you once again into His image.

The paradox, of course, is that in reality this has already been accomplished; you are the image of God. Christ's work was complete. Yet the baggage of our past and of our fears are daily being paraded before us by an enemy whose strategy now is to convince you that it is not true. So effective are his tactics that if you ask most Christians if they have any glory or greatness to their lives, they will likely respond with a rather self-righteous, "No, for 'I know that nothing good lives in me'" (Romans 7:18). They forget to include the second half of that verse, where Paul clarifies, "that is, in my sinful nature." It's our old self, our sinful nature, that is the "nothing good" Paul refers to. But now we are new creatures in Christ. "Therefore, there is now no condemnation for those who are in Christ Jesus, because through Christ Jesus the law of the Spirit of life set me free from the law of sin and death" (Romans 8:1-2).

In other words, through Christ you are free from the old nature. "And so he [God], condemned sin in sinful man, in order that the righteous requirements of the law *might be fully met in us, who do not live according to the sinful nature but according to the Spirit.*" (Romans 8:3–4 emphasis mine). Paul explains this a bit further in Galatians when he writes, "I have been crucified with Christ and I no longer live, but Christ lives in me" (Galatians 2:20). The good news, the gospel, is that we are born again, not just relationally with Jesus, but spiritually as well. We *are* new creatures.

It is this new creature that God is inviting into the story of your life. He knows what is really in you, and He redeemed you for just that purpose: to be the person you were always meant to be. As you examine your life, then, you should expect to identify times that your Father sought to draw out that which is truest of you. This usually is experienced in one of two ways: either as an "Aha!" moment or as negative reinforcement.

The "Aha!" moments are our favorites, and they are well worth noting, as they can offer clues about what we were created for. Usually they come rather unexpectedly, like a surprise phone call from a long-lost friend. That is exactly what they are: a lost or forgotten friend that life buried under a mountain of distractions.

THE HEROIC PATH

I had one of these "Aha!" moments some years ago, although I didn't recognize it as such at the time. Shortly after my fifteen-month-old son had been diagnosed with cancer, as Christmas approached, I decided to write a Christmas letter. It was mostly therapeutic, I suppose, but I also wanted to offer some hope to our many friends who were suffering with us.

My Christmas letter ended up being less about what was happening and more about walking with Jesus in the midst of crisis. The response from friends was overwhelming as they shared how this simple, single page had touched them.

I did not consider myself a writer at the time and had no dreams of being a writer. Yet writing that letter gave me life. I could hardly wait until the next Christmas to write another.

Surely you have had similar experiences—times when you were doing something, maybe even selfishly or self-servingly, and something in your spirit said, "Yes, this is me!" That is the Spirit of God living in you, drawing out life in you.

Sometimes, however, that same Spirit needs to apply a little corrective discipline. It's not punishment, mind you, although it is meant to leave a bitter taste in our mouths. Frequently such discipline seems to interfere with much of the fun in our lives.

I know a young woman who believes that every time she messes up, she gets caught. The first time she went out drinking with friends, her car got wrecked. The one time she ran a quick errand without her driver's license, she got pulled over. She has story after story like these. You may say it's just consequence or bad luck, and maybe it is. However, as a teenager this young lady had a prophetic woman of God speak over her life, declaring that God had called her to a level of purity that was above the rest, and that her sins would always be found out.

I believe there is something about the call of this woman's life that is so important and so unique to her that God's hand is heavy on her. In the words of Solomon, "The Lord disciplines those he loves" (Proverbs 3:12).

One of the most useful exercises we can engage in, then, is to look back at our lives, journal open and pen in hand, and ask Jesus to remind us of the times when we felt His hand. What were you about when you felt that "Aha"? How and where did you wander astray only to be rebuked by a heavenly Father who loved you too much to let you continue? Those moments are clues. They are times of God fathering you, guiding you as a hall of fame coach would, reminding you whom you were created to be.

Sabotage

God is not the only one who recognizes your potential, though. Satan well understands God's plans for humanity's redemption; hence, his relentless opposition to the work of Christ.

While our enemy is not omniscient, he is vastly experienced at identifying and attacking our strengths before we ourselves ever recognize them. The twenty-first chapter of 1 Chronicles furnishes an example. King David, the leader of Israel, had a clear anointing from God on his life. David had led God's people out of the tyranny and arrogance of Saul, and through many battles he had established the Promised Land as God's kingdom on earth. The quality that set David apart was his humility. Be it dancing in the streets or weeping over past sins, David's willingness to humble himself before God was his identifiable strength.

So it shouldn't surprise us that "Satan rose up against Israel and incited David to take a census of Israel" (1 Chronicles 21:1).

At first glance, David's head count seems rather benign. Censuses are important for kingdoms. It's essential for a nation to know the size of its population in order to plan for the future. Jesus himself recognized the usefulness of numbers; in illustrating the importance of considering the cost of discipleship, He used the example of a king with 10,000 men going to war against a king with 20,000 men.

But David was not preparing for battle, nor was he planning for the future of Israel. It appears that his only real motive was to stroke his own ego: "Look at what I've done." God responded by punishing Israel, and a guilt-stricken David repented of his action. Far from reflecting David's true identity, the census had served to pollute it. The count David had taken was in direct opposition to who he really was.

That is a large part of the work of our enemy. In the book of Job, looking in on the royal courtyard of our Lord, we overhear a strange conversation between God and Satan: "The Lord said to Satan, 'Where have you come from?' Satan answered the Lord, 'From roaming through the earth and going back and forth in it'" (Job 2:2). Apparently the Devil had been looking for something and he had found it in Job. He was looking for righteousness, for calling, for the stuff of greatness, in order to challenge and hopefully destroy it.

Even those closest to Jesus were not immune. Jesus warned Peter that Satan planned to sift him like wheat. Satan does this, attacks the very core of our being. However, the manner in which he sifts us can in itself be a clue to our place in the story.

What parts of your life keep getting sifted? What plans have you felt sure were from God, only to have them continually frustrated? Such experiences often lead Christians to conclude that God must be closing certain doors. No doubt He is at times, but often, if you start probing, you'll find that God has been repeatedly directing your life to those very doors.

Here's an observation: If you have ever felt a strong pull from God in a certain direction, but nothing worked out when you headed in that direction; if instead of an easy path, you encountered overwhelming setbacks and even danger; then you were very likely heading toward your own heroic path.

In times of opposition, it is easy to conclude that you've heard God wrong or perhaps are being led astray by your own pride. Trying circumstances certainly call for wisdom and time to listen closely to God. However, they also call for courage to walk through the dark places. Opposition doesn't necessarily mean you're wrong; it may mean you're so right that someone wants to stop you.

Look back at your "failed" ventures. Is there a pattern to them? Does it seem like each time you stepped out in an area of ministry or service or some other deep desire, it was opposed, or temptations became progressively more overt? Could these seeming failures in fact reflect your strengths, areas of potential glory in your life that Satan wants to squelch?

Pinpointing Your Location

We've considered two of the three factors involved in determining the unique path God has laid out for you. To recap: 1) How has God been shaping your character and life-calling? and 2) How has Satan attempted to prevent you from walking in what God has for you? Now let's look at the last leg on that three-legged stool: How can you accurately interpret the events of your life?

Interpretation can be a tricky thing, for nothing is ever what it seems. Remember those words of my old college statistics professor: "Figures don't lie, but liars can figure." You can manipulate the data to produce a variety of conclusions. So how do you interpret your life? "Did God say or did the Devil do?" has tripped up more than just a few godly men. Context is central to understanding the particular episode of your story that you are evaluating at any given moment.

You will need some coordinates. What you absolutely must not do is look only at what you can see in front of you. That vision is clouded—by circumstance, by experience, by both enemy and friendly fire. To get a true context for what is happening around you, you need a larger picture.

If you have ever used a GPS device, then you understand the importance of multiple satellite angles for pinpointing your position. One or two just won't do; but with three or even four, global positioning technology can locate your place on the planet within inches.

For Your Eyes Only

As a Christian, you have available to you a number of different satellites. Used in isolation, they can leave you more confused than confident. But combined, they have unheard-of power to identify exactly who and where you are. And in so doing, they can provide the context you need to accurately evaluate the events of your life.

Your first satellite is the written word of God, the Bible. Notice that I didn't say it was your only satellite. There are those who would say that the Bible holds the answers for all of your questions, and in a general sense, it does. But it doesn't tell you whether you should skip your son's swim meet to pray for a sick friend; it doesn't specify whether you should teach Sunday school or spend that time refreshing your own soul; and it certainly doesn't tell you what your choice in a career or a spouse should be.

The Bible does, however, develop a picture for you of God's perspective on all of these concerns. Moreover, it allows you to learn from others who have walked with God on paths similar to yours. Most importantly, it offers uncompromising truth concerning who God is and what He created you to be. The Bible is the plum-line against which all other input must be measured. Other satellites that contradict the written Word of God can be universally discarded as false signals.

This last principle alone can dramatically clear the playing field. God doesn't send mixed signals, so we can be confident that all other guidance must align with His Holy Scriptures. However, just knowing this is not enough. We all know that the Bible has been used to support some pretty awful things. We still need more input.

THE HEROIC PATH

Jesus made an incredible promise in the last hours before His death. "I will ask the Father," He told His disciples, "and he will give you another Counselor to be with you forever—the Spirit of truth … [He] will teach you all things and will remind you of everything I have said to you" (John 14: 16–17, 26). Our second satellite locator is the Holy Spirit. That Spirit is residing in you, and you would do well to tune in and listen to His advice.

The idea of listening to God speak within us raises red flags for many believers. Again, the potential for serious misguidance is evident. We've all followed the news coverage of different religious leaders who have done horrific acts "because God told them to."

Nevertheless, the Bible is full of examples of God guiding His leaders by the Holy Spirit. Hearing the Spirit is really a trained skill, much like learning to understand radio lingo in an aircraft. Unfortunately, many of us fail to learn how the Spirit speaks until a crisis forces us to listen. Our anxiety at such times often results from our lack of experience in listening. The key to hearing from God is to listen for Him daily in the little things of life—to develop a "conversational intimacy" with Him, as John Eldredge would call it. With so many voices in our heads, be they the world or our pride or the Devil, it takes time and experience to discern God's voice.

But again, we have other coordinates to help. Does the voice you're hearing align with the written Word of God? Is it consistent with what God has communicated to you in the past? Does it fit with your present circumstances? Apply these criteria as you make a practice of listening daily for the voice of the Holy Spirit and you will be surprised by what you hear.

I've just alluded to the third coordinate: a survey of where you are at this moment. An objective eye is critical here in order to honestly interpret the present part of your journey. Have you been following a call of God on your life, or are you, like the prophet Jonah, on the run? Are you dealing with issues such as pride, self-glorification, or a need for validation? What has God been doing with you during this season? Has this been a time of repentance, of fresh commitment, or of vision-building?

Don't gloss over this important evaluation of your present situation; spend some time honestly and deeply examining your current life. Piecing all of it together like a complex puzzle will help you form a picture that can further your understanding of the events surrounding you.

On to our next coordinate: fellow warriors. "Plans fail for lack of counsel, but with many advisors they succeed" (Proverbs 15:22). We will devote an entire chapter to the matter of bringing others around you later in this book, but the importance of doing so must be stated here.

As humans, we are naturally nearsighted. Whether we are being barraged by accusations, temptations, or failures or whether we are enjoying the accolades of the crowds, human nature is such that it is almost impossible for us to see our lives clearly without the perspectives of others.

As a self-proclaimed loner, I know how difficult it can be to cultivate solid, trustworthy relationships. We men are busy with our families, our jobs, and other time-consuming responsibilities. Oh for just a few moments of complete peace and quiet! Yet if we are

THE HEROIC PATH

determined to fight as men and fulfill all that God has called us to, then much will be required of us. And in order to remain properly oriented, we have got to establish a "satellite" of good comrades.

Choosing whom we will allow to speak into our lives is just as important as choosing to listen. Rehoboam, as he prepared to receive the kingdom of his father, Solomon, was immediately confronted with a rebellion (1 Kings 12). He sought counsel; however, he made a poor choice in his selection of advisors.

Rejecting the wisdom of the elders, he listened instead to foolish young hotheads much like himself—his ol' high school buddies, so to speak—and as a result, experienced the backlash of a divided Israel.

In our quest for wisdom, we need to find men who are not afraid to speak truth to us, regardless of how that truth may make us feel. Hearing the counsel of wise friends can leave us feeling overwhelmingly vulnerable at times. But cultivating relationships with men whom we trust enough to allow them to speak freely and honestly into our lives will pay incalculable dividends.

Some things really are too hard to understand. But much is not. Sometimes it just takes enough tenacity to look at the big picture of your life—the forest instead of the trees. What is God developing in you? What is the Enemy trying to destroy? Where are you located in the story right now?

Study and know God's unchanging Word. Listen to His Holy Spirit speaking in you. Look around you at your surroundings. And seek counsel. You will be amazed at the secrets that are revealed for your eyes only.

TRAIL MARKERS

1. Have you ever had an "aha" moment when you were doing something and found yourself thinking, "This is what I love. This is what I want to do"? What was it that you were doing?
2. Have you ever experienced the correcting hand of God? What might your Father been warning you of or saving you from?
3. What parts of your life keep getting sifted? What plans have you felt sure were from God, only to have them continually frustrated? What is Satan trying to stamp out in you through such recurrent opposition? How successful has he been?
4. How trained are you at listening to God's voice and knowing the truth of his Holy Scripture? Are you ready to begin developing that skill daily?
5. Where are you at this moment in the story? Are you following God's call on you or running from it? Are you on the front lines, or have you been evacuated to a MASH unit? What particular personal issues are you dealing with right now: pride, fear, self-identity, pain? Does your current situation make more sense as you consider such coordinates?
6. Do you have men who can speak honestly and openly into your life? Are you willing to seek out such men? If you're feeling brave, ask the men with you right now what they see in your life?

Chapter Eleven

Dreams, Desires, and Passion

*Dreams are like stars ... you may never touch them,
but if you follow them they will lead you to your destiny.*

Anonymous

*Delight yourself in the Lord and he will give you
the desires of your heart.*

Psalm 37:4

THE HEROIC PATH

Growing up in a small Midwestern town in the early 1900s was anything but glamorous. Most boys didn't finish high school, and fewer still ever ventured more than a few miles from their birthplace. But David (actually his middle name, after his father) was different. His parents insisted that he, together with his other brothers, not only finish high school, but consider college as well.

This was more than okay with David, who had applied his younger years on the prairie to filling his head with stories of the pioneers who had tamed the West. Their lives were the stuff of legends—and David's life was the beginning of one.

After spending a few years working to help pay for his brother's college education, David received an appointment to West Point Military Academy. During these years he learned to endure hardships, to persevere—and to lead.

Upon graduation, David was assigned stateside. The young second lieutenant served admirably, but he was growing increasingly aware of his personal dreams. David longed to be a warrior, like the heroes in the stories he had listened to growing up. He desired to be on the front lines, bringing peace and stability to a dangerous and often volatile world. Yet despite David's repeated requests to be deployed to combat duty, World War I was not to be his war. Instead, David was assigned to observe the War Department's First Transcontinental Motor Convoy—essentially, a bunch of broken-down, muddy trucks slowly making their way across the country.

But dreams—real dreams that is—never die that easily. Through the following years, the young officer worked his way up the ranks

Dreams, Desires, and Passion

and quickly gained recognition for his abilities. By 1935, he was accompanying General MacArthur to the Philippines as a military advisor. And then, on December 7, 1941, Pearl Harbor was bombed by the Japanese. Our warrior, Dwight David Eisenhower, now a brigadier general, was summoned to Washington.

World War II would be Eisenhower's war. A series of promotions eventually lead to the five-star rank of General of the Army as Dwight Eisenhower led the American forces on the D-Day invasion of Normandy—one of the most daring and successful "Wild West" adventures ever.

Dreams, desire, and passion: they molded and directed the life of the man who would eventually become the thirty-fourth president of the United States, and who years later would be ranked by C-Span as fifth (only behind Washington, Lincoln and both Roosevelts) in the area of moral authority.

Dreamers

Like David, I have dreams, and I know you do as well. I've dreamed of being a rock star, a daredevil, and a fighter pilot. I've imagined climbing great mountains and rescuing heroines in distress. I have pursued life goals, and in doing so have disciplined myself and given up lesser pleasures.

But time is the great enemy of dreams. Time has a way of crushing desire and snuffing out passion. Over time, dreams are lost and forgotten. Goals become utilitarian, pragmatic... sensible. Who has time to be a rock star or a daredevil when you have

THE HEROIC PATH

a family to support and responsibilities to manage? Abdicating such priorities to pursue personal gratification would not only be impractical, it would be immoral. So as years turn into decades, dreams die. And a part of us dies with them.

This is one reason why the infamous midlife crisis that many men experience can be so dangerous. A man sets aside many of his dreams in order to live a practical, logical life; then one day he realizes that his prime years are quickly fading. So he buys a motorcycle (I bought five), leaves his wife and children (almost did that one too), or worse. And as all of his attempts fail to fill the void, the man comes face-to-face with the ugly reality of unfulfilled desire: dreams that will never be.

Most of us leave our dreams and desires there, dead or dying in the desert heat. We look back and determine that they were the cause of our destruction and pain, so we do what any noble man would do: we walk away from them.

There is another option though. We can examine our dreams through the eyes of the One who created us with those dreams. "'For I know the plans I have for you,' declares the Lord, 'plans to prosper you and not to harm you, plans to give you hope and a future'" (Jeremiah 29:11). God, in His omniscient, creative power, made you for a reason. He planned you from the beginning and in doing so created you with unique dreams and desires, set in place so that you would find that place. In looking at those desires, we can begin to understand our role in God's great story.

Psalm 37 states that God gives us the desires of our hearts. There are two parts to this process. The first is the impartation of our desires, the placing of various passions in our hearts. God is their originator, just as He is the Creator of our entire being. True, our dreams and passions can get really messed up, polluted by the world around us and contaminated by sin, but that doesn't negate the fact that the original, uncorrupted versions were placed there by God. "For you [God] created my inmost being; you knit me together in my mother's womb" (Psalm 139:13).

The second part of Psalm 37 involves the fulfillment of the desires God sets in us. We play a crucial role in this part; it comes as the fruit of delighting ourselves in God. As we seek Him with all of our hearts, the desires we have always had, placed in us by God Himself, come to fruition.

But we are getting ahead of the story. Let's look more closely at the nature of desire.

Cryptographs

It is a worthwhile exercise to revisit the dreams you had as a youth. Don't edit, don't spiritualize, just honestly look at the things you dreamed of doing when you were ten years old, or fourteen, or twenty-one. Where did your mind escape to when it needed to get away from the noise and the chaos of a young boy's life? When you were alone or with your closest friends, whom did you pretend to be?

As you begin to chronicle those fantasies that you thought were just empty imaginations, you will likely begin to see a pattern emerge. It is part of a series of clues and speaks of a hidden truth.

THE HEROIC PATH

It is not so much a photograph as a cryptograph, a reality masked by the medium it is presented in. That's one reason why you can't base your life on just a single dream or desire: often that dream is only a part of the puzzle.

Some of my own boyhood dreams demonstrate what I mean. Early on, I was a huge fan of the British rock band The Monkees. (Wow, is that dating me or what!) Later my interest turned to the teen stars, especially Donny Osmond. I imagined myself being "found" by the Osmonds, perhaps as their long-lost brother, and joining them on the road, singing onstage as one of the Osmond brothers. Now, understand, I can't sing. And I hate concerts! Yet part of me longed to be in front of an audience proclaiming something.

Another childhood hero of mine was Evel Knievel. You remember that daredevil of the 1970s, dressed in an American Flag and jumping his motorcycle over cars, busses, even the Grand Canyon. I wanted to be like him! That dream is still a very real part of my life. It shows up in me as a love of risk and a desire to do things that have the potential for either greatness or utter failure. It largely explains why I am drawn to motocross racing, rock climbing, and jet skis.

At the age of thirteen, I visited the United States Air Force Academy in Colorado Springs. Instantly I was captivated by the airmen of the academy, especially the pilots. That, I decided, would be my career: I was going to be a fighter pilot.

My dad, an airman during the Korean War, was very supportive as I researched the requirements for acceptance into

Dreams, Desires, and Passion

the Air Force Academy. Good grades, extracurricular activities, and a recommendation from a state senator or representative—all became areas of focus for me. That is, until I went to my barber. Waiting to get my cut, I was excited to find a magazine article on the training of our military's fighter pilots. Then I read a single line that changed my life forever. It stated that pilots were required to have 20/20 vision.

I wore thick glasses.

Devastated, I set the magazine down. Yet God had awakened something in me through the entire experience. It was a desire to dare, to live on the edge, to pursue great dreams, and to fight for freedom.

Thirty years later, the dreams I have shared with you here are beginning to make sense (guess you could say that I'm kind of a slow learner). I understand with greater clarity God's purpose for my life. My boyhood dream of being onstage has ripened into my calling as a speaker and motivator. My love of risk is essential in ministry, a vocation that requires a man to lay much on the line while facing his own fears, others' doubts, and an enemy who opposes his every move. And my ambition to be a fighter pilot prefigured what God has invited me into today: a high-stakes battle for the freedom of many who have been taken captive by the Enemy.

Remembering What God Already Knows

Go back to when your heart was young, when responsibility and obligation weren't even a part of your vocabulary. If you can't remember such a time, then dream. If you had unlimited resources and no other expectations on your life, what would you love to do?

Of course you have responsibilities—that's understood. But just for a moment, forget them and look at what comes to the surface. What have you always dreamed of doing, of being?

Now filter those dreams through the new heart that Christ has given you. He's the One who knew you even before you were born. Consider God's words in this Bible verse: "Before I formed you in the womb I knew you, before you were born I set you apart; I appointed you as a prophet to the nations" (Jeremiah 1:5).

That sentence makes several amazing claims. For starters, before Jeremiah was even conceived, God knew him. Jeremiah was no afterthought, not one of those last-minute "Oops, now what do I do?" surprises. God had thought the prophet's life through in advance and knew who Jeremiah would be called to be. Such foreknowledge on God's part shouldn't be hard for us to understand. All-knowing and not bound by time or space, God would of course know each of us before we were ever formed. However, if we follow this reasoning through—especially given how often we wonder whether God has a worthwhile life for us to reach for—it raises a thought-provoking question. If God is love, and if all that He creates is good; if no evil or wasted effort is found in Him; and if He is the One who created us; then how can we imagine that we were *not* created for a significant purpose?

It is true that we were born in sin, and it is also true that God will give us over to evil ways and hardened hearts if we choose

Dreams, Desires, and Passion

them. But such choices and the failed dreams that result from them do not reflect the future that God had in mind for us.

The second statement of the Jeremiah verse is that God not only recognized the prophet, but also set him apart long before he ever breathed Earth's oxygen. The Father looked at Jeremiah while he was still in his mother's womb, much like He looked at His only begotten Son, Jesus, in Mary's womb. And God dreamed, as any good father would do, a dream for Jeremiah's future. As a father myself, I know what such dreams are about. My wife has delivered four beautiful babies into our family for us. With each one, during those nine months of waiting and excitement, as my wife endured the nausea and experienced some of the strangest cravings I have ever seen, I dreamed. I dreamed of who each child would be, what he or she would look like, how I would love that child, what I would name my son or daughter.

Like me, "You're at least decent to your own children. So don't you think the God who conceived you in love will be even better?" (Matthew 7:11, The Message). Imagine God during your gestation, almost giddy with excitement, knowing all that He has planned for you, all that He hopes for you!

But God is not just a dreamer. He's also a Creator. He sets worlds in motion. And so, having appointed Jeremiah as a prophet, God gave him authority and opportunity and education and experience to become what God desired.

God does so for you also. To the Christians in Ephesus, Paul wrote, "For he [God] chose us in him [Jesus] before the creation of the world to be holy and blameless in his sight" (Ephesians 1:4).

THE HEROIC PATH

Read that passage again, but replace it with your name: "God chose _____ in Christ before the creation of the world to be …" It is *you* whom God knew not only before you were born, but even before the creation of the world. He saw you not as a mess-up or a disappointment, but as a son, holy and blameless—in other words, exactly what He had dreamed of. Not just the Jeremiahs, the apostle Pauls, or the Billy Grahams, but also you and I have been placed here on this planet to walk in a dream and a purpose specific to each of us.

That dream is there, deep inside the heart God has given you. It is a major reason why He found it so important to send His Son, Jesus, to redeem that heart. It is of great, great value to the kingdom, because the King Himself created it with great value.

Search your heart and awaken its desires. Ask the One who created you to reveal the truth about that heart to you. "Search me, O God, and know my heart; test me and know my anxious thoughts. See if there is any offensive way in me, and lead me in the way everlasting" (Psalm 139:23–24). What you find could be absolutely life-changing. And as Dwight David Eisenhower discovered, the war that you thought you missed may have simply served to awaken the general who is destined to change his world.

TRAIL MARKERS

1. Which dreams have you left "dead or dying in the desert heat"? How do you feel about losing them?
2. Think back and list all of your past dreams that you can remember. Not just the ones to "bring glory to God," but the simplest, the silliest, the unobtainable ones of your youth. Do you see any commonalities among them that suggest a theme or themes?
3. If you had unlimited resources and no other obligations, what would you love to do?
4. Filter your childhood dreams and your answer to question number three through your three "GPS coordinates": where are you right now, what is God doing with you, and in what area of your life has the enemy attacked you?
5. Complete this statement, even if you don't fully understand all of your dreams and passions: "God chose [your name here] in Christ before the creation of the world to be ___."

Chapter Twelve

Just Do It

A beautiful thing never gives so much pain
as does failing to hear and see it.
Michelangelo

Go ... Surely I am with you always,
to the very end of the age.
Matthew 28: 19, 20

THE HEROIC PATH

If man's greatest fear is failing, then his greatest enemy is that fear. Few things can take the legs out from under the strongest of men like the fear of falling face-down in the mud and muck in front of everyone. That fear can castrate a man, leaving him impotent and unsure whether he is even a man at all.

Fear is the reason why most men research the information and read all the latest reviews on a new car or computer before they buy it, even if they already know which one they want. They're not so much motivated by the desire to make a good choice; they just want to make sure that they, the mighty hunters of North America, won't get ridiculed for making a bad one.

Fear is also why I dread walking into a jewelry store. It usually happens on occasions like the day before Valentine's Day or Christmas or a birthday. I think the sales lady at Zales must have some kind of super-hero radar that can detect my complete ignorance about any rock that's too small for me to rappel from. Or maybe she just keys in on my dilated pupils, sweaty palms, and nervous tic as she approaches me with that smile and soft tone that say, "Hello, sucker! You're about to double my commission today."

The reason for my apprehension is simple: I don't want to purchase something that would cause my wife's friends to look and then comment about what a Neanderthal she has for a husband. I want them to admire my choice and imagine Bond, James Bond. The problem is that I know, and I'm pretty sure the sweet little thing behind the glass case knows, that I have the fashion sense of a great ape. So I'm an easy mark. Convince me that every girl wants one, keep the price within two to three times of my budget, and you've got me.

I know men who have never set foot in a jewelry store, or a Victoria's Secret, or even a doctor's office for fear of looking like a fool. I know even more men who have never taken a step in fulfilling their God-given destinies because of that same fear. Their inaction isn't a matter of rebellion or selfishness. If they knew what God had called them to, they would pursue it. If Jesus showed up at their shoreline, asked them to cast their net on the other side of the boat, and then invited them to leave all and follow Him, they'd respond without hesitation. The difficulty is that Jesus hasn't done so, or at least they haven't heard Him.

The pain and bewilderment of not knowing what God wants, the risk of perhaps going the wrong way—of picking the cubic zirconium instead of the princess cut—leaves countless men forever standing outside, looking in through the large plate-glass window, paralyzed by their own uncertainty.

We've spent the last few chapters discussing how you can identify and follow God's call on your life as you develop some coordinates by which you can navigate. However, you and I would be quite naïve if we were to think that now all is clear. You may in fact be experiencing more confusion than ever. Satan certainly doesn't want you to hear any clear message from headquarters, so it is likely that a lot of excessive radio chatter has you feeling as if you have no clear direction to proceed in. But the tragedy would be for you not to go at all.

THE HEROIC PATH

Chaos, Confusion, and Conquest

In AD 66, as the early Christian Church was just beginning to develop a structure and a following and the Jews of Jerusalem were becoming increasingly unhappy with Roman rule, a rebellion began which eventually lead to Titus, the son of Roman Emperor Vespasian, destroying the temple in Jerusalem and murdering thousands of Jews. Many were forced to flee for their lives. No doubt there was little time for the Christians of that day to stop and pray, seeking God's direction as to which way to run; yet as they dispersed, the gospel was also dispersed throughout the known world.

A thousand years earlier, three young men from Judah had a comparable experience. Captured by the Babylonian army, Hananiah, Mishael, and Azariah were bound and, against their will, carried from their homeland to a foreign land. They were forced to eat strange food, observe unusual customs, and serve a king well known for his brutality. I doubt that much of their circumstances made sense to these three youths, and I can almost guarantee that not one of them felt he was fulfilling his destiny.

But then King Nebuchadnezzar issued his famous decree: "Bow down to my image." Shadrach, Meshach, and Abednego (the young men's new Babylonian names, no doubt still another source of shame) knew what they had to do. They could compromise on some things, but this command of the king was not one of them. Serving the king was one thing; worshiping his god was altogether different. They would not bow down to any god but the one true God. Their refusal should have cost them their lives. Instead, it changed a tyrant's heart.

Just Do It

As the young men safely exited the fiery furnace into which they had been thrown for their insubordination, Nebuchadnezzar looked at them in astonishment and declared,

Praise be to the God of Shadrach, Meshach and Abednego, who has sent his angel and rescued his servants! They trusted in him and defied the king's command and were willing to give up their lives rather than serve or worship any god except their own God.

Therefore I decree that the people of any nation or language who say anything against the God of Shadrach, Meshach and Abednego be cut into pieces and their houses be turned into piles of rubble, for no other god can save in this way (Daniel 3:28–29).

WOW! Talk about destiny and purpose. Those three young men couldn't have scripted their parts better if they had tried. And that seems to be the point: they didn't try. In fact, all that they really did was go with the flow.

Sometimes, that's all we can do too. While I believe that God delights in revealing His plans to His people,[6] nevertheless the Old and the New Testaments both make it clear that God frequently accomplishes His greatest feats through people who, at the time, have no idea He is using them and no sense of what is going on behind the scenes.

A good friend of mine once was trying desperately to discern God's direction for his life. This man was a devout follower of

---

6 See Amos 3:7.

our King. An opportunity came for him to move his family to a new location with a better job. As the Scriptures advise, my friend sought the counsel of others concerning this big decision. A group of us gathered around him and his wife, and together we asked God what He would have for them.

Not just once, but repeatedly, over months, we asked and prayed and begged for direction. None was given. The door remained open, and no one had any large concerns in their spirit. But neither did anyone receive an affirmative answer. The lack of any clear guidance produced turmoil in my friend's soul. He only wanted God's heart for himself and his family, and he became paralyzed by not knowing it.

Finally, in what was probably our twelfth discussion on the matter, I assured my friend that God was even more committed to His direction for him than he was. I encouraged him to take the position he had been offered, trusting that God would continue to walk with him. My friend did and God did.

The Heart of a Father

We must understand this about our Father: He loves us and He delights in our success. Where did we ever get the idea that God is trying to trick us into making some dreadful choice, at which point He will then disinherit us or bring disaster on us or who knows what? Nothing could be farther from the truth.

We get a picture of our King's heart in His first miracle during His life on earth. It's an odd story. In the second chapter of John, Jesus, attending a wedding banquet, is approached by his mother.

Just Do It

She explains that the family throwing the party has a somewhat embarrassing problem. It seems that they haven't adequately planned for so many people (or maybe they just never had the means to begin with). Whatever the reason, they have run out of wine.

Now, if you are the Savior of the universe and you are about to launch the most important, world-changing ministry in history, do you really want your first public event to involve alcohol and a party and some poor joker's lack of planning? Any first-year marketing student can tell you that this is probably not the best of ideas. You know that the *Jerusalem Enquirer* is going to run the story the next day: "Self-Proclaimed Messiah Parties through the Night."

Jesus likewise recognizes the poor timing of the request when He replies, "Dear woman, why do you involve me? ... My time has not yet come" (John 2:4). But Mary understands the heart of her God, perhaps because she has come to know it through the heart of her son. She tells the servants, "Do whatever He tells you." Jesus gives them instructions, they obey, and His first public miracle produces upwards of 180 gallons of some of the finest wine Galilee has ever tasted. Now that's a party!

Why does He do it? Certainly many of the revelers have already had more than enough to drink—hence the statement made by one attendant that usually the good wine is served first; then, after the guests have had too much to drink, the cheap stuff comes out. The answer comes in verse 11: "He thus revealed his glory, and his disciples put their trust in him." God loves to come through. In our weakness and failure and lack of perfect planning or perfect means, He loves to reveal His glory.

THE HEROIC PATH

And as He does, we learn to trust Him for the next thing, and the next, and the next.

"Therefore I tell you, do not worry about your life, what you will eat or drink; or about your body, what you will wear. Is not life more important than food, and the body more important than clothes? Look at the birds of the air; they do not sow or reap or store away in barns, and yet your heavenly Father feeds them. Are you not much more valuable than they? Who of you by worrying can add a single hour to his life?

"And why do you worry about clothes? See how the lilies of the field grow. They do not labor or spin. Yet I tell you that not even Solomon in all his splendor was dressed like one of these. If that is how God clothes the grass of the field, which is here today and tomorrow is thrown into the fire, will he not much more clothe you, O you of little faith? So do not worry, saying, 'What shall we eat?' or 'What shall we drink?' or 'What shall we wear?' For the pagans run after all these things, and your heavenly Father knows that you need them. But seek first his kingdom and his righteousness, and all these things will be given to you as well. (Matthew 6:25-33).

Seeking God, pursuing Him: that's what my friend was doing. Even though he had no clue what God was saying, he was earnestly trying to walk in His ways, and as he did so, God was directing his tracks. What loving father wouldn't? What father would give a stone instead of bread? What father with Special Ops training

Just Do It

would stand by and watch his untrained son get gunned down in a robbery without stepping in to help?

Your Father loves you. Stop for a moment if you need to and let that sink in. You may even want to put this book down and find a place to meditate on that single sentence. *Your Father loves you.* Maybe your earthly father loved you or maybe he didn't, but God, your heavenly Father, loves you intensely. He would turn water into wine for you. He would produce the catch of a lifetime for you. He would clothe you as a king. He has called you His son.

God isn't out to trip you up. He's on your side. He delights in your success. When a desperate father came running to the feet of Jesus with his demon-possessed son, unable to find anyone who could help his boy, Jesus assured him that "everything is possible for him who believes" (Mark 9:23). Ah, but there's the problem: believing. There's always a catch, the fine print of the faith contract. The boy's father realized he was busted. But instead of turning away, he dropped to his knees and pleaded, "I do believe; help me overcome my unbelief!"

Notice what Jesus didn't do. He didn't say, "Well, you're close. Go home, pray a little longer, learn to trust Me more, and then let's meet again in a few years and we'll see how your doin'." Of course not. He stopped, rebuked the spirit, and set the man's son free. Why? Because that's what love does.

So come on. What are you waiting for? It's just a door. Turn the knob and take a step inside. Stop looking in through the window. If the move you make is honoring to God, He will honor it; if not, He will gently redirect it. Your job is to just do it.

TRAIL MARKERS

1. Are there situations like my jewelry store experience that leave you anxious, even paralyzed? What are they, and why do you think they affect you?
2. What about personal, spiritual, or ministry decisions? How confident are you in hearing God's voice in them?
3. Your Father loves you. Stop and let the weight of that reality sink in. Wrestle with it for a moment. What thoughts, emotions, fears, doubts, or expectations is it producing in you right now?

Chapter Thirteen

Sitting at the Master's Feet

Experience: that most brutal of teachers.
But you learn, my God do you learn.

C. S. Lewis

Joshua said to the Israelites, "Come here and listen
to the words of the Lord your God."

Joshua 3:9

THE HEROIC PATH

The sport of rock climbing is a bit of an enigma. Most people recognize the inherent danger of holding on to the edge of a rock hundreds of feet in the air.

Yet many who have dabbled with indoor climbing at the gym or performed easier, guided climbs, having tasted only the elementary side of climbing, have a hard time grasping the extreme difficulty of the upper grades. So when you tell a non-climber that you climb, you often get a comment like, "Oh, yeah, my six-year-old niece does that at the local YMCA. Looks like a lot of fun."

They totally don't get it.

Bouldering is a specialized form of climbing. No ropes are used, as the athlete is usually only fifteen to twenty feet off of the ground and has a small, padded "crash pad" to land on if he falls. The idea is to do short bursts of extremely difficult moves. To aid in understanding the skill level required, each "boulder problem" (as they are called) is assigned a "V" grade. V0 is the easiest, with V16 being the current hardest-of-the-hard. Only one person (at the time of this writing) has attained V16—one young man who stands at the top of the climbing world, capable of that impossible climb. His name is Daniel Woods.

To understand the enormity of Daniel's skill, you need to appreciate that if I were to take you out to a rock, untrained but in reasonable shape, after a day or so you could probably climb a V0. In a few months you would likely be sending some V2s. Most people seem to stall out around V3 or V4. I know climbers who have climbed for years and never completed a V4. You see, the scale is designed to get exponentially harder—which makes the story of Woods's girlfriend, Courtney, all the more spectacular.

After meeting on Facebook, Daniel and Courtney began dating and quickly became very close. Courtney, a typical weekend climber, was sending V2s with some difficulty. Then she began climbing and training with the master of bouldering. He taught her technique. He showed her how to get stronger. Daniel explained the importance of focusing all of one's mental energy on the task at hand. And you know what happened? This pretty young girl from Tennessee was sending V8s within a year, something most climbers would be thrilled with as a lifetime achievement!

How did Courtney do it? The answer is obvious: She is in love with Daniel. She is spending every possible moment with him, watching, listening, learning. In the climbing world, she is living in the shadow of greatness—and it shows.

Jesus the Lover

Oh that we could all be Courtneys! Oh that we could all be so enthralled with our Lover, Jesus, that our every waking moment would be spent sitting with Him, eating with Him, learning what makes Him tick, listening to His wise advise, and sharing our failed attempts with Him, knowing that He longs to take us to the place He alone has ascended to.

My son, himself a skilled and accomplished climber, would give almost anything for that kind of time with Daniel Woods. If Daniel were to invite him along, he would leave in a moment.

"Call to me and I will answer you and tell you great and unsearchable things you do not know." (Jeremiah 33:3)

Our Master has invited us on such a journey. He has offered to be our Lover, inviting us to live with Him, to learn how He thinks, what His passions are, His priorities, His dreams … for us. Jesus has offered us a place of intimacy with Him, a place where we can rest our weary heads one moment, then the next moment train until our muscles are so fatigued that we can't take another step.

That closeness with our Teacher is where most of us miss the mark. Too often we view Jesus—God—as distant. Sure, He left some really great ideas with us in His "instruction manual," and there are a few good people out there who actually seem to understand His thoughts. But for the most part, we're on our own. If we really want to send that V8 boulder problem, we're just going to have to figure it out ourselves.

Even many of us who believe in personal communication with God see Him more as a consulting service or a scheduled personal trainer than a Lover. We set aside our thirty minutes a day, or maybe a Sunday morning, or even an occasional retreat as our time to listen. "I'm kinda busy today, Lord, but I can give you till 8:45. Shoot! What's the plan?"

"I Am with You Always"

Walking with Jesus does involve His guidance and training. But it's also about more than that, so much more. As our Christ was ascending into the heavens, not to return again physically until the end of the age, He wanted us to understand that He wasn't really leaving us. "Surely I am with you always," He said (Matthew 28:20). It wasn't hyperbole; He meant it. Wherever life leads us, whatever we are doing, whether we win or lose, Jesus is there with us, always. So it would behoove us to learn to sit at His feet through all of life's experiences. How else can we hope to cultivate the kind of relationship that can lead us to the battlefront—and maybe even back in retreat— while orchestrating our victory?

It is said that the best way to learn a foreign language is not to study it in school, but rather to move to the country of its origin and immerse yourself in that place—its culture, its smells, and the nuances of how its people talk.

The same is true of our Jesus. Yes, we need to study about Him. We need to learn the theology of our faith. But we need more; we need to be with Him daily, hourly. Not just during the good times, but also during the bad times, the sinful times, the absolutely ungodly times, the times when we fall face-first off of the rock, bloody our faces, curse His name, and vow never to climb again.

After all, it's not like He's not already there. You didn't think He would leave you during those times, did you? "Surely I am with you always"—remember? That wasn't a conditional statement. Jesus hasn't changed His position. He's still there. Sit with Him, even in the filth and the shame.

This is a hard concept for many of us to grasp. How could Jesus stay with us during our times of failure? That's one of the

THE HEROIC PATH

great questions that the Pharisees had of Jesus, who frequently dined with sinners, refused to condemn a woman caught in adultery, and even in his last moments on the cross promised a repentant thief a place with Him in paradise. That's just the way Jesus is: merciful. So share your frustrations, your anger, and your disappointments with Him. He won't turn away from you.

I believe that same attitude of acceptance and love in Daniel Woods is what pushed Courtney so quickly up the skill ladder. Most climbers, when we are at the gym or the crag, tire too quickly. We head home, rest, sleep, play. But when you are with Daniel Woods, well, going home is not an option. You're gonna be on the rock all day long. You are never going to climb as hard or as strong as Daniel does, so the only choice is to deal with your failures and your frustration. But the cool thing is, Daniel knows exactly how you feel. He's been there. He's experienced the same disappointments.

Besides, Daniel is just as in love with Courtney as she is with him. And "love covers over a multitude of sins" (1 Peter 4:8).

In that same way, Jesus is in love with you. "He will take great delight in you, he will quiet you with his love, he will rejoice over you with singing."[7] He invites you to His table as a son of the Father—no longer a servant but a friend. More specifically, an heir of God and co-heir with Christ. As such, Jesus invites you into daily, intimate relationship with Him.

---

[7] Verse references for the second through fourth sentences of this paragraph, in order: Zephaniah 3:17, John 15:15, and Romans 8:17.

Mephibosheth

There's an interesting story in the book of 2 Samuel. As David was establishing his throne and living in the shadow of great victories, he asked a strange question for someone in his position: "Is there anyone still left of the house of Saul to whom I can show kindness for Jonathon's sake?" (2 Samuel 9:1).

While a kind gesture, it was also a dangerous one. Once an heir of King Saul was found, a good argument could be made that this person was the rightful successor to the throne. David's inquiry also put Saul's grandson in a dangerous position. Having spent the last several years in hiding, poor Mephibosheth risked assassination if he showed his face.

Still, David found him, brought him out of hiding, and restored all of his wealth. Moreover, the narrator tells us that "Mephibosheth ate at David's table like one of the king's sons" (2 Samuel 9:11).

What a picture of our King's invitation to us! Once His enemy, we by all rights should have been sentenced to death. Instead, He welcomes us as one of His own, invites us to come and dine with Him, and seats us with Him by the very throne of God.[8] One day we will be the rulers and leaders of His eternal kingdom, a truth the Scriptures bear out time and time again.

The question then becomes, why wouldn't He lead and train us? And why wouldn't we desire to be lead and trained? So often we forget that we are children. Yes, we may have walked with Christ for

---

[8] Verse references for this sentence, in order: John 17:22; Revelation 3:20 and Psalm 23:5; and Ephesians 2:6.

a number of years, and we may have developed a certain maturity to our lives in Christ. But really—mature? Why do we insist on assuming that we should have "arrived" by now? Isn't that notion really pride? And isn't pride the very thing that God opposes and Satan uses to trip us up time and time again? We are, every one of us, being molded daily. And that process isn't always smooth sailing.

Sitting at the Master's feet: That is where true transformation happens. That is where heroes are crafted. That is where David found himself time and time again in all kinds of circumstances. Running for his life, David cried out to God to rescue him from those who surrounded him. Guilt-stricken over his murderous affair with another man's wife, David threw himself at the mercy of his King. Marching the Ark of the Covenant into his newly established kingdom, David danced unashamedly before God as a child might before his daddy. And in Ziklag, after months of working for his enemy, turning his back on God's plan, when it all fell apart, "David found strength in the Lord his God" (1 Samuel 30:6).

All Things

Should we be any different? Jesus promised that He would not leave us alone, but would give us a new Companion, His Holy Spirit, who "will teach you all things" (John 14:26). That guarantee covers a lot of ground, "all things." Like, what do you do when you're so mad at your wife that you could just spit? Or how about those times when you're exhausted and just can't take another step? God hasn't come through for you, and frankly, you don't care if He does. "'F' this whole thing." Do you really think God is surprised by your emotion, by your lack of etiquette, by your foul mouth? Are those times not included in the "all things" clause?

It may be in the victories that we fail the most. When we win, when we succeed, there can be an incredible sense of power and success. Everything we touch turns to gold, and it can become so easy to just start charging ahead. David faced that one too:

> When the Philistines heard that David had been anointed king over all Israel, they went up in full force to search for him, but David heard about it and went out to meet them. Now the Philistines had come and raided the Valley of Raphaim; so David inquired of God: "Shall I go and attack the Philistines? Will you hand them over to me?"
>
> The Lord answered him, "Go, I will hand them over to you."
>
> So David and his men went up to Baal Perazim, and there he defeated them. (1 Chronicles 14:8–11)

Sounds pretty straightforward, wouldn't you say? The problem was, the Philistines didn't take defeat well. They decided to attack again. No need to fear, though; obviously God was on Israel's side. David knew now that he could defeat the Philistines. Just charge the front again, right? Wrong. David again asked God what to do. "God answered him, 'Do not go straight up, but circle around them and attack them in front of the balsam trees'" (1 Chronicles 14:14).

THE HEROIC PATH

That is what a student does, even when that student is the great warrior David. He asks his Guide, his King, what to do. No assumptions, no living on past victories, no dwelling on repeated failures. David demonstrates a lifestyle of walking intimately with God in all things, every step of the way.

How would your life be different if you lived by that same motto? Most of us tend to wait until the "big" decisions need to be made before we inquire of God, often as a last resort. Unfortunately, during those times, when we are pressured and stressed and need an answer *now*, it becomes very difficult to discern God's voice from the thousand other voices of our friends, spouse, the world, and the Devil. Heck, even the pizza from the night before might be talking to you.

Such high-stress situations are a bit like having someone assign you to an F-16 fighter jet and then send you into a dogfight. You don't even know where the eject button is, let alone how to fly the thing. So it is with many of our spiritual battles. We run in headlong or get drafted against our will, then suddenly realize we haven't the foggiest notion what to do.

But what if today we began training our ears to hear God? Running away from God in Ziklag, basking in a God-given victory, in bed with our best friend's wife, preparing for battle … regardless of our situation, now is the time to open up communication with God; now is the time to begin the dialogue.

Don't worry if you don't hear anything, or if this business of communicating with God makes you feel extremely uncomfortable. God doesn't mind. He just wants to hear your heart. He wants to walk closely with you, His son. He has invited you to his table not on your own merit, but rather out of His love of you.

That's the great lesson of the Mephibosheth story. David brought Mephibosheth into his home out of a promise he had made to Mephibosheth's father, Jonathon. Later in the story, as David's own son Absalom attempts a coup, there is a question as to whether Mephibosheth has been faithful to David or sided with Absalom. David doesn't even ask Mephibosheth if the rumors are true. He simply dismisses the matter as if nothing had happened (2 Samuel 19). Why? Because David had made a promise to Jonathon and to Mephibosheth. And in a like manner, God has made a promise to you: "I am with you always."

David's love must have had an incredible impact on Mephibosheth. Daniel Woods's love certainly is having an impact on Courtney, whom Daniel incidentally has recently married. Why not sit with your Father, your King, through your day today. Invite Him into your greatest and your worse moments. You will be amazed at how much stronger your climb becomes. Living in the presence of greatness has that effect.

TRAIL MARKERS

1. What has your approach to learning from Jesus been: more like He's a lover or more like He's a paid personal trainer?
2. When is it hardest for you to "be with Jesus"? During a defeat? In the midst of sin? When life is turning up all roses and you are '*winning*'? (My apologies to Charlie Sheen.) Why do you find it hard to approach Jesus at those times? Where do you think He is?
3. Why do you think King David was able to repeatedly turn his heart to God even during his worst failures?
4. What are the occasions when you feel as if the "all things" clause in John 14:26 doesn't apply to you?
5. Training Moment: Quiet your heart for a minute. Shut off the cell phone, turn down the TV, grab a cup of Joe, and ask Jesus to speak to your heart. Don't worry if you don't hear anything; just pay attention to where your heart and your emotions go. What clutter and radio chatter is keeping you from hearing Jesus? In the midst of it, can you find a morsel of peace or a calming of your spirit? That's Jesus!

Chapter Fourteen

Bandages, Splints, and Other First Aid

Foremost among the many problems that can compromise your survival ability are medical problems resulting from unplanned events, such as forced landing or crash, extreme climates, ground combat, evasion, and illness contracted in captivity.

Many evaders and survivors have reported difficulty in treating injuries and illness due to lack of training and medical supplies. For some, this led to capture or surrender.

THE HEROIC PATH

Survivors have related feelings of apathy and helplessness because they could not treat themselves in this environment. The ability to treat yourself increases morale and aids in your survival and eventual return to friendly forces.

One man with a fair amount of basic knowledge can make a difference in the lives of many.

U.S. Army Survival Guide, Chapter 4, Basic Survival Medicine

It is not those who are well who need a physician, but those who are sick.

Jesus, Luke 5:31 (NASB)

Bandages, Splints, and Other First Aid

What's a guy to do? Mo was raised in the finest of homes. His mother adored him, showering young Mo with nothing but the best—the finest education, the latest designer clothes, meals fit for a king. His father, a great leader and motivator, carefully shaped and sculpted his younger years as Mo learned the value of hard work, the significance of a good name, and the responsibility of overseeing multi-million dollar projects. When Mo walked into the work place, heads turned. A handsome young man with the confidence of a prize fighter, Mo also had a kindness and compassion about him which reassured his subordinates that they were not just employees, but friends.

Mo was living the dream. He was going to make a fine catch for some lucky lady one day.

But all of that changed one hot, humid summer day. After reviewing his company's workforce and labor practices, some inconsistencies began to surface. Uncertain whom to blame, Mo, always the manager, addressed the issue. That is, after all, what he had been trained to do. He was a leader. The company would one day be his, and he was not about to inherit a corrupt business. So he had to let a man go. Middle management is always hard to deal with anyway, and when it interferes with smooth production … well, the decision seemed obvious enough.

Unfortunately, Mo's father didn't see it that way. He feared a full investigation by the union. The workforce likewise felt threatened, interpreting Mo's actions as an attempt by Mo to gain more power.

So it was that Mo found himself sitting alone at a dusty, smoke-filled local watering hole, contemplating what to do next.

THE HEROIC PATH

His father had fired him, vowing never to allow him within miles of his former life, and rumors of Mo's incompetence had spread like wildfire throughout the entire business community. Mo was honestly just trying to do the right thing—okay, maybe with just a bit of a chip on his shoulder, but come on. Within just twenty-four hours he had single-handedly managed to destroy the only thing he had ever known.

Mo had another drink. Numbing the past seemed the only viable thing to do. He would go on, he would find something else. "If they don't appreciate my skills, who cares. Forget them all." Mo got up, dusted himself off, and started walking.

He didn't even notice the gaping wound in the center of his chest.

Gaping Wounds

Mo's story certainly is not unique. It may be a bit more dramatic than yours or mine, but then again, not really. The wounds that we have received and will receive ... well, they can change everything. In an instant. And most of us do with them exactly what Mo did. We go on. We don't bandage our injuries. If we seek any treatment for them at all, it's usually a little anesthesia in the form of a bottle or a burger or the Internet. Otherwise, we just keep moving.

What else can we do? The past can't be undone and the opinions of others won't change. Bridges were burned. There's no going back, so we go on.

The problem, of course, is that we really don't go on. We run. We settle for second best. We find something, or someone, to

Bandages, Splints, and Other First Aid

make us feel better about ourselves. We ignore the depth of the wound that is still there, oozing, festering, affecting every choice that we make.

In fact, we begin to make agreements with the wound. Agreements like,

"I was never meant to do that in the first place."

"I will never try that again."

"They deserve what they get."

"Why bother. My time is better spent elsewhere."

Maybe it's true. Maybe you *were* in a place or a job or a situation that was over your head. But behind such words lies a larger and more pathological agreement: "I will never risk again."

That vow, my friend, can leave you treading water in the middle of life's ocean when what you should be doing is building a raft with the wreckage of your previously prized cabin cruiser.

Wounds need to be treated. In my years of medical practice, I have often witnessed the results of injuries left untreated: small splinters that became infected, gangrenous, and eventually required amputations. Large, easily repairable lacerations that were left to heal on their own, leaving hideous scars and loss of function. Dirty abrasions that were never properly cleaned, leading to sepsis and making weeks of debridement and intravenous antibiotics the only option.

The first step in treating a wound is to recognize its seriousness. I'll never forget a patient I once had. He called the office reporting that he was injured—didn't make it sound like a big deal, but wondered if he could maybe be seen that day. My receptionist put him on the schedule.

THE HEROIC PATH

When the man's appointment time eventually arrived, he was sitting calmly in our reception area. He told my nurse, nonchalantly, that he had cut himself and thought that he might need a tetanus shot.

When I got with the patient, the truth quickly emerged. The man had a six-inch stake impaling his scrotum! Talk about stoic! I'd have been crying like a baby. After hours in the operating room, the surgeon was optimistic that at least one of the man's testicles could be salvaged.

It's easy to downplay our failures and wounds. "It's not a big deal" is easier—not to mention more macho—than admitting that we really screwed up and got ourselves into some deep doo-doo. There is something that seems honorable about minimizing our personal pain. Maybe it's that whole John Wayne thing, or maybe it's a false understanding of humility. Whatever it is, it doesn't help.

But you're thinking, "I don't want to be *that guy*." You know—the guy who is at the altar every week, always bringing up his wounds, blaming all that he is or is not on what has happened to him. You offer compassion, maybe a few prayers, some good practical advice, but it never seems to stick. Eventually, he just wears you out. You begin avoiding him, quit answering his calls, and vow never to be like *that guy*.

I'm not suggesting that you should become that guy. Self-pity can be just another manifestation of selfishness. I am suggesting rather that you acknowledge the truth, and the truth is that you are in a battle and, like most combat soldiers, have sustained some wounds. Maybe you took a bullet to the leg, slowing your walking. Perhaps shrapnel has blinded one of your eyes, or maybe the constant recoil of your own rifle has deafened you to the point where you can no longer hear your commanding officer's orders. Then again, prolonged battle may have affected you psychologically. Post-traumatic stress disorder (PTSD) can render you confused, angry, and unable to engage anything. Whatever the problem is, one thing is true: until the condition is brought out in the open and you make peace with whatever permanent losses you've endured, you will continue to place both yourself and your comrades in harm's way.

Medic!

Unfortunately, revelation is not restoration. Merely acknowledging your wounds is never enough. Something needs to be done about them. This is where the medics come in.

I pulled one of my dumbest stunts a few years ago. I ignored a splinter in my foot for several weeks until it eventually became permanently embedded in the skin of my sole. Every step caused pain to shoot though the whole of my foot. I knew that a simple procedure could take it out, but I didn't want to bother my partner with the product of my own negligence. So I did what any doctor would do: I decided to take it out myself.

Sitting down on a stool in our procedure room, I grabbed a syringe and injected the sole of my foot with lidocaine. After repeatedly pulling away from the pain of the needle, I eventually succeeded in anesthetizing the operative site. With my legs crossed and a scalpel in hand, I began the delicate task of carving out the foreign body. That's when the bleeding began—a *lot* of bleeding. Without an assistant in the room, I was forced to stand up and hop on my one good leg to the opposite counter, trailing blood as I went, in an attempt to find a hemostat and cautery to stop the hemorrhage.

By the time I located them, the pain from the injection, the heat of the summer, and the sight of my own blood had dropped my blood pressure to that of a squid. I envisioned my nurse walking in a few hours later to find me lying on the floor in a pool of my own blood, my hands still grasping the weapon of my own destruction. (Did I mention that I had closed the door so no one would know what a moron I was?)

I'm happy to report that I didn't pass out. I was able to stop the bleeding, remove the splinter, and patch myself up. Then, after a few cool compresses and a glass of water, I mopped up the whole mess and no one was ever the wiser. But that was just a small cut on my foot. When we are wounded, really wounded, it becomes difficult for us to think clearly.

So if you've been badly wounded, find someone who *can* think clearly. Talk to your pastor or a good friend. Find someone who is unbiased, who has the courage to tell it to you like it is; someone who will grab the bleeder and hold pressure, even if you do pass out.

If need be, seek professional help or join a recovery group. Do something. There are a lot of good, highly qualified resources available out there. Use them. Sometimes all you really need is a different perspective, an unbiased party sitting on the outside

Bandages, Splints, and Other First Aid

looking in who can empathize with your situation and hand you the Neosporin.

Seeking this kind of help can make us feel incredibly vulnerable. We men are taught to suck it up, to fix our own problems. "Never let them see you sweat," has become the mantra of men sitting at the poker table of life. It takes courage, real courage, to pursue the life support that you need. A little perspective helps as well.

Remember my earlier story of Aron Ralston, the climber who had to cut off his own arm. There is a scene in *127 Hours,* the movie about his experience, when Aron has finally cut himself free and is walking the eighteen miles back to his car. Starving, dehydrated, having lost a large amount of blood, and on foot in the desert heat, Aron is far from over his ordeal. This cocky young man who previously had needed no one, who would take off on a whim and felt he had the world at his beck and call, suddenly realizes that he is not the superman he had thought he was.

That's when he sees a couple of hikers: a man and woman and their child. A week earlier, Aron wouldn't have given them a second thought. They certainly aren't the extreme athletes that he is. But now ... well, now Aron's perspective is different. Aron begins crying out like a child, first with barely a whisper, but then louder and louder: "Help me ... please ... *help me!* HELP ME, I'M HURT!"

I hope that likewise your own perspective has been changing as we've walked this journey together. You're not rock climbing at the local YMCA; you are experiencing the most extreme of circumstances. Trying to gut it out in silence just won't do; the consequences are tremendous. Your wounds are critical, even life

THE HEROIC PATH

threatening. This is no time to play Rambo; this is real life, not some Hollywood fantasy. Get help now, please. We need you.

Operating Room

Once the bleeding is controlled and the pain has been numbed, you're by no means ready to jump back onto a rock. You need a good surgeon.

"I have heard your prayer and seen your tears; I will heal you." (2 Kings 20:5)

There comes a place in our journey, a fork in the road, where we must decide which path to travel. One path seems quicker, flatter, maybe a bit safer, but it does not lead to healing. It is unfortunately the road that too many of us take. On it, we learn to adapt. We don't have to give as much of ourselves, and given the gravity of our wounds, this road seems the better option.

A true warrior, however, will never take that road, for it does not lead back into the battle, and the battle is what he was created for. The hero instead chooses the path to the infirmary; the athlete begins rehab; and the servant of the King seeks out the Great Physician.

It is in the presence of Jesus and His mercy, and only there, that you will find the healing that is crucial if you are to complete your journey. Certainly you can skip this part. Once the acuteness of the pain wears off and the embarrassment begins to fade, you can go on as if nothing ever happened. Many men do. But if you join them, your unhealed wounds and unresolved issues will

Bandages, Splints, and Other First Aid

plague you. Your enemy will use them to castrate you of your courage, and in the end you will be less than you were meant to be—and less than you desire to be.

If ever a man needed healing, it was King David. He was a great leader and a bold warrior. He was handsome, charismatic, and extremely talented. But he had also been wounded multiple times in the course of his life. The rejection and murderous attacks of King Saul ... David's personal failure to protect his own men ... the contempt of his wife, Michal ... his incompetence as a father ... the ugliness of his multiple moral failings ... if you take all the pomp and glitter out of David's story, the pages of his life read like the account of a man lying on a psychiatrist's couch, explaining to his analyst why he can no longer go on.

But David did go on. What was his secret?

In Psalm 30, David writes, "I will exalt you, O Lord, for you lifted me out of the depths and did not let my enemies gloat over me. O Lord my God, I called to you for help and you healed me. O Lord, you brought me up from the grave; you spared me from going down into the pit" (Psalm 30:1–3).

David knew where to find healing. He understood that in order to lead the people of Israel and fulfill his God-given purpose, he needed to have his wounds not just bandaged, but healed. And he recognized that only God, the One who created him in the first place and placed him on his journey, could make him whole again.

Nothing else defines a man of God more than this: his willingness and determination to give Jesus free rein in restoring him back to the man he was meant to be. That is, after all, what our

THE HEROIC PATH

Lord came to do, isn't it? "He [God] has sent me [Jesus] to proclaim freedom for the prisoners and recovery of sight for the blind, to release the oppressed, to proclaim the year of the Lord's favor" (Luke 4:18–19). And isn't that what we see Him doing throughout His time on earth? Calling failures and outcasts to Himself, restoring prostitutes, giving second chances to murderers and thieves, even placing those who had rejected him in charge of His ministry once He left planet Earth. Reread those gospel stories again. Each time, with the precision of a surgeon, Jesus carefully dissects the scars and restores the patient once more to a state of health.

You can experience that same kind of transformation yourself beginning today. Jesus is just waiting for you to ask and to take the uncomfortable, exposed road to the foot of the cross to receive your healing. Your journey may take weeks, months, or even years, but restoration can be yours.

Mo's healing took forty years, during which time he tended sheep in the mountains near Midian. It was there that he saw the burning bush. "So Moses thought, 'I will go over and see this strange sight—why the bush does not burn up'" (Exodus 3:3). Moses investigated and God spoke, telling Moses to take off his sandals because he was standing on holy ground. Then God did what God does: He healed Moses by reviving his vision for his life. "This is what you are to say to the Israelites: 'I AM has sent me to you'"(Exodus 3:14).

Mo had blown it the first time. His intentions might have been good, but his timing was terrible. Not this time, though. This time God was sending him—restored, healed, and with authority.

Bandages, Splints, and Other First Aid

God wants to do the same for you, you know. Doesn't matter where you've been, what you've blown, how presumptuous or pigheaded or cowardly you were—this time is different. This time, not only in spite of, but perhaps even because of your failure that has driven you to the foot of the cross, the great I AM wants to send *you*.

TRAIL MARKERS

1. Have you ever received a wound that you chose to ignore, walking away and vowing to never put yourself in a similar position? What was that wound?
2. What wounds or failures have you downplayed, convincing yourself that they were no big deal?
3. Do you have a medic in your life, a man with whom you would feel safe sharing your wounds? Who is he? If you don't know such a person, how can you find one?
4. "Nothing else defines a man of God more than this: his willingness and determination to give Jesus free rein in restoring him back to the man he was meant to be." Let's begin the process with this prayer: "Jesus, I believe that You created me for a purpose, a purpose uniquely mine which is needed at this moment in time. But life has been brutal, my glory has been shamed, and I have been unable to walk out this glory. Much of it I have just abandoned, laying it aside in an attempt to make peace with my own disgrace. Restore me, Jesus. Heal me, Jesus. Repair my gaping wound and begin my rehab. I place myself in the competent hands of the Great Surgeon."

Chapter Fifteen

Instrument Rating

Are you tired of being grounded due to cloudy skies and that one patch of cloud hanging right over your airport? Do you want to go above the clouds and enjoy sunshine while people at ground are getting drenched in rain? If so, it is time to get Instrument Rating.

PilotOutlook.com

For we walk by faith, not by sight.

2 Corinthians 5:7 (KJV)

THE HEROIC PATH

GPS technology saved my marriage—or at least my honeymoon. Uh, make that my second honeymoon.

Sandra and I were married in 1983. I was nineteen and she was twenty. We had seldom traveled outside of the small rural county where we both grew up. Without a lot of money but with an abundance of hope and adventure that come with teenage love, we set out on our first married adventure together: a honeymoon at a Best Western in Kansas City, Missouri. Heading out in our Ford Fairlane 500 (a six-hundred-dollar car my parents had given us as a wedding present), we planned to spend a day at Worlds of Fun and then Oceans of Fun before heading back to Nebraska to start our new life together.

Kansas City is about six hours from my hometown of Norfolk, Nebraska. It was the middle of June and temps were in the upper nineties, with humidity close to the same. Our "new" Ford didn't have air-conditioning, but it did have power windows—and they were rolled all the way down!

It was dark and late when we arrived in KC. I had driven on a freeway maybe twice prior to that day, so I was no road warrior. The traffic was buzzing. Signs identifying this exit and that bypass flew by like bats startled from their slumber as my bride tried her hardest to read a map to a city we had never visited. I was just trying to keep us alive. Hands glued to the steering wheel, I hollered above the noise of the traffic and wind coming through our open windows, "Where do we turn?"

"I'm not sure. Which road did we just pass?" Sandra said.

"How am I supposed to know what road. I'm driving! Look at the map!" I fired back.

"I think that may have been the exit there," she replied as we continued on, unable to change lanes. Tired, hungry, hot, and just generally being the jerk that I tend to be, I grew increasingly impatient, and before long Sandra and I were experiencing real married life. The honeymoon period was apparently already over, and we hadn't even reached the hotel.

Fast-forward twenty-five years. Finances were better, the kids were grown, Sandra and I had somehow managed to survive that first disappointment as well as many others, and now we were taking a real honeymoon, a second honeymoon, this time to Hawaii.

Landing in Honolulu International Airport, we rented a small car, another Ford. And then I did what can only be described as genius: I opened my suitcase, produced the Garmin GPS that we had brought from home, and turned it on.

"Acquiring satellites," it said. We waited a few moments. "Enter destination." I pulled out the hotel brochure and carefully keyed in the address. "Turn left in 500 feet."

"M," as I am fond of calling the British voice that is programmed into my GPS, directed us right to the doorstep of our honeymoon suite. No arguments, no snide remarks, no stopping and asking directions. It was beautiful.

Sandra and I didn't have a single argument about directions that entire trip. I had learned to trust my GPS, and it didn't disappoint. It was faithful in directing every turn we made.

THE HEROIC PATH

The road that you are traveling can be just as confusing and frustrating. It is so easy to overlook an exit or misread a map. Simply choosing to get back on the road, to begin walking once again with your God, and even to receive the healing that you so desperately need, can still leave you feeling more than a bit frazzled when your destination is unknown and the path unfamiliar. Worse yet, if you try to proceed the way you did decades ago, or maybe just weeks ago, without the updates to the technology that time has produced, you may find the same old issues resurfacing.

But that's the beauty of time. Too many people live with regrets—regrets over lost opportunities, failed attempts, and wasted years. But the time that has passed has served a purpose. It has molded you, updating your technology, if you will.

> Consider it pure joy, my brothers, whenever you face trails of many kinds, because you know that the testing of your faith develops perseverance. Perseverance must finish its work so that you may be mature and complete, not lacking anything. (James 1:2–4)

Through all the years, God has been in the business of molding your faith. I know it may have seemed like He wasn't there. Maybe you even told Him to leave, or perhaps He gave you over to your sins, allowing some hard and painful lessons. Maybe this side of eternity honestly looks like He abandoned you at the very time when you needed Him and were depending on Him the most.

But He was there. And there are lessons that He wants you to learn from those passages in your life.

20/20 Hindsight

An excellent way to start is to look back and review those times. If you were a professional athlete, most athletic trainers would encourage you to keep a journal of your workouts and performances. In it you would record not only how each workout went, but also how you felt during the workout, what you were thinking before and after, what the weather was like, and who you worked out with. The more details, the better. Not just achievements, either; the journal needs to include the good, the bad, and the absolutely ugly.

The beauty of these journals isn't apparent when you're writing them. Their magnificence surfaces months and even years later, as you review and make note of what worked and what didn't work. It's in retrospect, after you've had a few really bad sessions, that the notes you've taken start to shine.

That's what experience does for the man of God. He looks back at the good and the bad places in his life and evaluates where God, his faith, the Enemy, and even his mindset where during those times. Remember, "In all things God works for the good of those who love him, who have been called according to his purpose" (Romans 8:28). That's you. You are the one who has been called according to God's purpose, and God is in the business of training you through each event of your past, regardless of what it looked it.

I have a "collection." None of it is valuable and some of it is downright junk, but I protect it like it is gold. Among the items are an old set of dog tags, a wrinkled pit pass to a NASCAR race, and an old glass pickle jar.

THE HEROIC PATH

The dog tags were my dad's. He gave them to me when I was a young boy, and they were among my most valued possessions. One day, as I was exploring an area around my neighborhood of about nine square blocks, I lost the tags. I felt sick at heart. Searching frantically for the tags, I began to realize that my chances of finding them were almost zero. That's when, in the middle of a large field on the side of a hill, I began praying, crying my heart out to God. The dog tags were so important to me.

As I prayed, tears forming in my eyes, I chanced to look down. There at my feet, buried under the summer grass, were my dad's dog tags. I gaze at them now and remember that the things that are important to me, regardless of their importance in the world, are also important to God.

A number of years ago I took my youngest son Josiah to his first NASCAR race. He was a huge fan of Jeff Gordon, so to complete the experience I had ordered a pit pass on the Internet. But when we arrived, we were informed that our pass was not for that day. I felt like a complete failure as a father. I had never checked the date.

I don't know about you, but I am always hesitant to ask God to intervene in front of my children. I guess I'm just afraid that He won't, and then how do I explain His lack of response to them? So I prayed, but silently. No luck. Josiah and I were not going to get in. Looking Josiah in the eyes, I took a big breath and suggested that we pray together for someone to have a pass for us. The move felt so risky, so exposing. What if God didn't come through?

Instrument Rating

I don't like to be the center of attention, so I wasn't about to stand on a chair and scream that I needed a pass. My son and I simply walked around quietly and began asking people if they had a pit pass they would like to sell. I tell you, not more than five minutes later someone came up to us and said he had a couple of extra passes. He gave them to us, no charge!

As we walked onto pit road, whose car was being inspected but number 24—Jeff Gordon's car! Josiah handed his hat to the pit crew and the entire team signed it.

Had my son and I gone down to pit road earlier when we had first tried, Gordon's crew wouldn't have been there. Even now I am getting chills thinking of how my God honored my willingness to trust Him in front of my young son.

And then there is the pickle jar. On it are written the words "Ode de two-stroke." The jar was a Christmas present. A good friend who was as obsessed with Jet Skis as I was knew that the winter months left me with no opportunities to ride. So before heading over to our home one day, he went out into his garage, started his Jet Ski, and filled the jar with two-stroke exhaust fumes. When we opened it in our living room, the whole house smelled like a summer day at the lake.

My friend's simple act reminded me that God has blessed me with some great people in my life who will go to great and absurd lengths to bring a smile to my face.

Those and other trinkets remind me of the faithfulness of my King. He is on my side. Yes, God is busy running the universe, juggling the planets, influencing world events, and advancing His kingdom. But He is also walking with David Kortje daily.

It's not just the warm fuzzies that remind me of His companionship. The dark times, the lonely times, the times when I have knowingly rejected His ways, and the times when my prayers haven't been answered as I had hoped remind me also. I can look back at each of those times and, with the clarity of 20/20 hindsight, see how my Father was holding me, or just waiting for me to return to Him.

Counselor God

"Now faith is being sure of what we hope for and certain of what we do not see" (Hebrews 11:1).

That sureness, that certainty, doesn't just happen. We cannot convince ourselves into faith. We cannot study it enough that it becomes ours. I don't care how many times your jump instructor reassures you that the parachute will catch you, that first jump out of the plane is still gonna make you pee your pants. Experience is the great teacher of faith.

So Jesus, as He was preparing to leave this earth, offered us some help. "And I will ask the Father, and he will give you another Counselor to be with you forever—the Spirit of truth … [he] will teach you all things and will remind you of everything I have said to you" (John 14:16–17, 26). Think William Wallace reminding the Scots why they should fight and not run, or Rocky explaining to his estranged son that his son is better than that, referring to his son's willingness to settle for less than he was. It is in walking with the Holy Spirit, and in reviewing where we have been and what God has been up to in our lives, that we discover the faith we need for the moment. We can't manufacture such faith; we can only receive it.

Opportunity Knocking

The problem with faith is that it is so fleeting. You may enter the championship game filled with passion and confidence, certain of your victory. But two quarters and twenty-one unanswered points later, your earlier "assurance" begins to look pretty silly. That sort of awakening is no doubt where a lot of men are today. It's where I am much of the time. Such experiences are times of truth—"the times that try men's souls," as Thomas Paine wrote during the American Revolution. I understand that these situations may seem like disappointments or setbacks. But they are really opportunities that can't be manufactured or bought; rather, they must be seized.

Responding to opportunity is your next step. You absolutely must risk again. There is no easy way around it. Each time you act on an opportunity, all of your past failures and disappointments will be there "reasoning" with you why you should avoid taking the risk. But the Holy Spirit will also be present. And if you listen for Him, He will remind you of all that God has done and all He has promised.

Like a car teetering on the edge of a great canyon, your ability to fly by faith—to further develop your instrument rating—hangs in the balance. Some men are content to play it safe, to stay on the ground until the clouds clear. But if you've made it this far in the book, I doubt that you are one of them.

What is it that God has called you to? How can you take a risk today? Maybe the risk you need to take involves a phone call or an important conversation. Maybe it's financial or work-related. Perhaps a habit or even a chronic sin needs dealing with. Or maybe you, like me, need to simply sit down at your computer and start writing, unsure if anyone will ever read your stuff. I don't know what risk looks like for you, but I do know this: unless you take that step and risk failure and embarrassment again, you will never get a chance to walk on pit road.

Experience is your friend. Your GPS is more accurate today than it ever was.

Maybe it's time to take that second honeymoon.

TRAIL MARKERS

1. What are some of the hard lessons that you have learned through the years?
2. Can you look back with 20/20 vision and identify times that God was fathering you?
3. How are your faith and your experience with God different than they were ten or even five years ago?
4. What risk, what step of faith, do you need to take today? What are the lies and the agreements you've made with the past that keep you from taking that leap?
5. You are not the same man today that you were yesterday. Are you willing to trust Jesus with the real you?

Chapter Sixteen

Covering Your Backside

To fall in love is easy, even to remain in it is not difficult; our human loneliness is cause enough. But it is a hard quest worth making to find a comrade through whose steady presence one becomes steadily the person one desires to be.

Anna Louise Strong, American Journalist

A friend loves at all times, and a brother is born for adversity.

Proverbs 17:17

THE HEROIC PATH

American poet and novelist May Sartan once wrote, "Though friendship is not quick to burn, it is explosive stuff." Ain't that the truth!

Most men struggle with friendships. I certainly do. It's not that I don't want friends or value them, because I do. It's just that … friends are so messy. They take effort, a lot of effort. One minute they want to watch a football game with you; the next, they need help sodding their yard; the next, they are in a crisis. Add to that their daughter's graduation party, the cordless drill they never returned, and a good dose of Jones-envy that you feel each time your buddy gets another promotion, and it can just seem easier to do life by yourself.

It's not that we don't want friends. We just have so many other demands on our lives—work, spouse, kids, church, and chores—that it can become very easy to let the whole friendship thing slide. Especially if you tend to be an independent introvert like me.

I was trained to believe that independence was a good thing. "Learn to do things yourself" was the underlying message I picked up from school, work, the media, even home. "Just don't be a burden" is my unspoken mantra. Some of my self-reliance is noble, but honestly, a lot of it is just plain selfish. I don't want to have to deal with anything else—or anyone else.

A few days ago, a family friend offered to change the oil in my daughter's car. She was more than happy to take him up on the offer. Unfortunately, her front-wheel-drive Suzuki has two drain plugs close to each other, and the friend drained the transmission fluid instead of the engine oil. Ten miles down the road, my daughter's free oil change transformed into a $7,000 transmission replacement.

My daughter feels overwhelmed; the friend feels terrible; and the friendship—well, to say it is strained would be putting it mildly. Our friend offered to pay, but how can we expect that of him? He was trying to help our daughter, not harm her. As for me, my thoughts have been, "Why didn't you just let me do it, or a garage? Then at least we wouldn't have a friend to blame."

I'll say it again: friendship is messy. And if we have established one thing throughout this book, it is that life is already messy enough. It doesn't need any help. So for me at least, it's easier to keep friendships at a minimum.

Islands

The problem, as the poet John Donne wrote in "Meditation XVII," is that "no man is an island." We were created for relationship just as the Godhead eternal exists in the relationship of Father, Son, and Holy Spirit. By virtue of being created in God's likeness, we require community as part of our image-bearing nature.

Solomon, the king of great wisdom, demonstrates the value of relationships clearly and practically in Ecclesiastes, chapter 4:

Again I saw something meaningless under the sun:
There was a man all alone;
he had neither son nor brother. There was no end
    to his toil,
yet his eyes were not content with his wealth.

THE HEROIC PATH

"For whom am I toiling," he asked,
"and why am I depriving myself of enjoyment?"
This too is meaningless—
a miserable business!

Two are better than one,
because they have a good return for their work:
>   If one falls down,
his friend can help him up.

But pity the man who falls
and has no one to help him up!
Also, if two lie down together, they will keep warm.
But how can one keep warm alone?
Though one may be overpowered,
two can defend themselves.
A cord of three strands is not quickly broken.
>   (Ecclesiastes 4:7–12)

The truth is that as messy and demanding as friends sometimes are, we need them. We need them to teach us how to love. We need them to provide direction and purpose in our lives. We need them to keep us from going mad. And we need them to cover our backsides.

Let's just state the obvious: you will not become all you were meant to be, your life will not attain its full impact, without some very close, loyal friends. Comrades in battle are not just a luxury, they are a necessity. Despite the work and friction of friendship, good friends will be your lifeblood, and you, theirs.

The "just me and Jesus" mindset doesn't cut it in real life. Yes, Jesus is your closest friend. He will never leave you and will never disappoint you. When all others have abandoned you, He will still be there and will walk through the darkest of times with you. But even Jesus recognized our need for earthly, flesh-covered friends. He developed a group of twelve around him, modeling the relationships they would need for the persecution that was to come. He sent them out in twos for a reason. He gave Paul, Barnabas. He gave Moses, Aaron; and Adam, Eve. David had Jonathon, Nathan, and Joab—a prince, a prophet, and a general.

Splinters and Vows

Which brings us to our first point: friends can come from any area of our lives. They may be coworkers, subordinates, spiritual mentors, or spouses. They may be just like us or very different from us. Friendships may be made in heaven or they may be full of friction. The important thing is that friends are honest and committed to us, and we are committed to them.

That's really the kicker, isn't it? Commitment. Because quite honestly, most of us have been burned by a trusted friend at some point in our lives. So we have become calloused. Guarded. Hardened. Nothing sears our heart like the betrayal of a friend. When someone we love and trust turns against us, or abandons us, or just quits calling, it does something inside us. Frequently that something manifests in the form of a vow. It may be unspoken or even unrecognized, but it is there, like a splinter, reminding us of the pain whenever we get close to putting pressure on the spot again.

That pain leads us to decide, either consciously or subconsciously, to never try again. We make superficial friends, we are cordial, but once a relationship begins to develop and a little conflict or exposure surfaces, we sabotage the connection. The pain of the splinter becomes unbearable, the memories of past wounds haunt us, and so we run. Sometimes by simple avoidance; other times by busy distractions or just shutting down completely; occasionally by sudden, unexplained anger and outbursts—in various ways, the friendship grows distant. And once again, we become an island.

If what I've just described sounds like your own life, allow me to offer some advice from one who has faced the same struggle, and still faces it frequently. That is the enemy. That is Satan. He wants to sabotage your life, and you must stand against him. You must fight his efforts to isolate you. To do so, though, you need to explore how one fights these battles. Let's begin by understanding how Satan gets the weapons he uses.

It all stems from the vows we made when we were wounded the first time (or the tenth, or the hundredth). Vows are simply agreements we have made with ourselves. Yet they are more than just agreements; they are promises.

God takes vows very seriously. In Deuteronomy, He declares: "If you make a vow to the Lord your God, do not be slow to pay it, for the Lord your God will certainly demand it of you and you will be guilty of sin. But if you refrain from making a vow, you will not be guilty" (Deuteronomy 23:21–22).

Our enemy likewise holds us to our vows. They are an open door for him. Paul tells us, "Do not let the sun go down while you are still angry, and do not give the devil a foothold" (Ephesians 4:26–27). Vows provide footholds for the Enemy. Like splinters, they cannot be ignored. They fester, and the closer we get to their source—in this case, relationships and friends—the louder they scream at us to get away, until eventually our only recourse is to retreat.

This is why Jesus made such a big deal about forgiveness. "For if you forgive men when they sin against you, your heavenly Father will also forgive you. But if you do not forgive men their sins, your Father will not forgive your sins" (Matthew 6:14–15). I don't believe that Jesus was trying to make our forgiveness conditional as much as He was driving home a point: unforgiveness builds a wall around us that traps us in our own issues and subsequently thwarts the plans God has for our lives.

I recently experienced this is a very tangible way. A number of years ago, I met a man who made a huge impact on my spiritual life. He challenged me in my faith, pushed me to pursue God, chastised my sin with love and understanding, and reminded me regularly of my Father's heart for me, his son. This friend became like a brother, and I trusted him with some of my deepest hurts.

Then a few years ago, something strained our friendship. My friend was struggling with some of his own pain, and as I attempted to bring it out of him, he pushed me away. (At least, that is how I perceived his actions through the fogged-up windshield of my own past vows). My friend's response hurt. It rubbed against a splinter of abandonment and betrayal that I have had for years. Whenever I tried to approach the man, the splinter dug deeper, more painful than before.

The only thing to do was stay away. It was easier. It was more comfortable. My friend and I were still cordial; I didn't speak poorly of him, or he of me. But there was a wall between us. At first it was barely noticeable. It was actually rather reassuring. Safe, even. However, as it continued, God began to reveal how it was affecting my life. I wasn't walking in the passion I had felt before. There was a guardedness to my life and my ministry. The Enemy began telling me that my message was not needed, and I began questioning my calling. Apathy snuck in under the guise of distractions until finally my heart needed to either surrender its passions to my enemy or else I needed to fight. "Guard your heart, for it is the wellspring of life" (Proverbs 4:23). I needed to fight for my heart.

So I called my friend. We sat down over coffee, and I apologized for the distance that I had built and the judgments I had made of him. Explaining to him how I had interpreted his actions, and acknowledging that I had very possibly misread them, I told him of the pain that I had experienced in our relationship. And I forgave him for it, regardless of his motives.

Almost immediately, a weight lifted from my shoulders. It was as if a heavy backpack—one I had carried for so long that

I no longer realized how much it slowed me down—had been suddenly removed. I felt energized, alive again! The stronghold had been destroyed. The Enemy had fled. Life was restored.

The only way to fight the darkness of relational injuries is by bringing the wounds, the pain they caused us, and the vows we made in response into the light. We do so through the medium of forgiveness.

It has been said that forgiveness is not about the person being forgiven, but about our ability to release the anger and disappointment we carry so that we can move on. I couldn't agree more. I'm still careful in relationships, and I'm still not ready to walk in complete, bare-all openness with the man I mentioned above. But I have released my grudge, and that is where the cleansing starts.

Strong and Courageous

Beyond forgiveness, friendships need to be pursued and fostered. This is really what separates the men from the boys, the posers from the pros. If you have been wounded by rejection, by failure, or by success; if you have convinced yourself that you need no one or that everyone is untrustworthy; then cultivating a friendship may be the most dangerous mission you ever step into. The reason, of course, is that you may fail. The friendship could blow up in your face, leaving you to emerge on the other side wounded one more time, possibly looking like a fool or maybe just feeling downright pissed off. It takes incredible courage to get back onto the same wild horse

THE HEROIC PATH

that threw you the last three attempts. But that is exactly what I am recommending you do: cowboy up and risk again.

> Joshua said to them, "Do not be afraid; do not be discouraged. Be strong and courageous. This is what the Lord will do to all the enemies you are going to fight."
>
> (Joshua 10:25)

Make no mistake: isolation is your enemy. Not the people who've hurt you, but the temptation to make yourself into a self-protective island; the separation, the self-reliance, and the I-don't-need-anyone attitude. These things are your enemy which ultimately will destroy you—unless you fight against it with courage and strength.

This life was never meant to be lived without friends. This battle was never meant to be fought without comrades. Your kingdom will never advance without a round table of trusted warriors by your side.

The thing that I find interesting about all of the "strong and courageous" passages in Scripture is that they are all calls for action. Notice that they don't say, "Pray for strength and courage," and they don't tell you to wait until you feel strong and courageous. They simply say, "Be strong and courageous." Acting on that exhortation is a step of faith a man takes knowing that there are no alternatives.

A few weeks ago, a young boy climbed over a fence into a leopard cage at our local zoo. The large cat came at him, wrapping its paws around his head as people looked on in horror, paralyzed in fear for the young child. Except for one man. He didn't know the boy, but he immediately recognized the danger. Without hesitation, he jumped the fence and began kicking the animal until it let go of the child.

Later, in a local television interview, this hero retold his story. He didn't feel like a hero and said that if he'd had to think about it, he probably wouldn't have done it. He had just reacted to the need of the moment.

That is courage: simply acting on what needs to be done. You can't over-think these things. The scenario above could have turned out much differently for both the man and the boy, and your acts of courage may turn out differently than you hope. Nevertheless, you must act. And the good news is, you have an excellent reason to believe that the Creator of the universe will smile on and bless your acts of courage. You have a reason to be strong and courageous: "The Lord your God goes with you; he will never leave you nor forsake you" (Deuteronomy 31:6).

But the first step is yours.

Created For This

Not only do you need friends, you also need to be a friend. You need to fight for those who will fight for you. Walt Whitman wrote: "Comrade, I give you my hand, I give you my love more precious than money, I give you myself before preaching or law; will you give me yourself?" All men feel the effects of war. All struggle just like you. And all need your hand just as you need theirs. Make a decision to be there for them—not to judge or preach or correct, but rather to lend your strength to their struggles. As relationships grow, your friends may in fact invite your counsel. Right now, though, what they need—just as you do—is a comrade to fight for them and alongside them.

Please don't miss this incredible opportunity. "Greater love has no one than this, that he lay down his life for his friends" (John 15:13). And here's the good news: you want to do this. You were created to do this. Isn't self-sacrifice what makes all the great movies and books so captivating: a man giving his best on behalf of someone else, sacrificing his time, his energy, or even his life for a friend? Such nobility doesn't happen by accident. God created us in His image, and His image is one of sacrificial giving.

One of the easiest ways to offer yourself in this fashion is to simply keep your ears open and your eyes peeled. Men are notorious for not asking for help, but they love to talk about all the work they have to do. The next time you hear a friend chatting about the shed he needs to build or the dishwasher that broke down, tell him you would love to come by and lend a hand. Don't let your offer sound like charity. Instead, mention that your friend's project is one you've wanted to learn more about or something you simply enjoy doing. Let your friend think he is doing you a favor by inviting you into his world.

Another great equalizer among men is coffee or even a beer at the local sports bar. Yes, I know that many Christians frown on the use of alcohol. But let's face it, men lay down a lot of their posing in non-religious settings. Sitting down with a man outside the atmosphere of I'm-gonna-fix-you opens up some of the deepest friendships because they are honest and real. Not agenda-oriented, just relational.

You might also consider inviting a man to help you do something. Sure, you could do it yourself, maybe even faster. But your vulnerability in asking for help diffuses that man's awkwardness. Besides, you might actually learn something.

One last suggestion: allow each friendship to evolve naturally. Don't sit down with a man the moment he shows up and begin sharing the Four Spiritual Laws or exposing your greatest fears and needs. Rather, give the relationship time to grow and mature. On the other hand, if your friend gets honest with you about his wounds, then listen with compassion. Don't try to fix him; just listen, empathize, and leave him with the assurance that you are available whenever he needs to vent.

Hey, look, I know this is all perilous territory. Like leading a brigade through a mine field, it will take every bit of courage you can muster, and through the journey, you will likely experience more failures and wounds. But on the other side, when your comrades have seen your commitment and bravery, you will have cemented a foundation of loyalty that only the great ever achieve.

TRAIL MARKERS

1. What has been your experience with friendships? Have you had some really good ones? Some really bad ones?
2. Can you recognize any vows you have made in the past concerning friends and relationships? What were they? Try to put them into words. How do they affect your friendships today?
3. How do you feel about forgiveness? Is there anyone whom you need to forgive so that you can move on?
4. What are some ways right now that you can step back into the arena of friendships with strength and courage?
5. Take a pen and write down the names of a couple of men whom you will call this week. No big agenda. Just call and see how they are, or maybe meet them for coffee or a movie.

Chapter Seventeen

Weapons Training

If the Union is once severed, the line of separation will grow wider and wider, and the controversies which are now debated and settled in the halls of legislation will then be tried in fields of battle and determined by the sword.

Andrew Jackson

Put on the full armor of God so that you can take your stand against the devil's schemes. For our struggle is not against flesh and blood, but against the rulers, against the authorities, against the powers of this dark world and against the spiritual forces of evil in the heavenly realms.

Ephesians 6:11–12

THE HEROIC PATH

Today is Father's Day. I really don't like Father's Day; it feels like Valentine's Day to me. You know: one of those days when others are supposed to be kind to you and tell you what a great person you are. It just doesn't seem very genuine under those circumstances. Because if there is one area in my life in which I have failed over and over, hurting those who are closest to me, it is in the area of fathering.

It's not like I try to mess up. In fact, I really do try to be a great dad, offering wisdom, understanding, encouragement, and discipline while trying to give enough freedom to grow and enough boundaries to protect. The problem is that in the midst of life—in the midst of the battle, when bullets are flying and tempers are flaring—all of my good intentions seem to get jumbled into one of those small, nuclear dirty bombs that contaminate and destroy everything in their immediate vicinity.

My other problem with Father's Day is that it is always on a Sunday. I suppose that for non-church-goers this is a good thing, but for those of us who profess Christ and still believe in the gathering of believers, well, the sermon can be painful. For some reason I have never understood, it seems that while pastors love to use Mother's Day as a chance to encourage and uplift our better halves, on Father's Day they declare open season on all of a man's deadbeat tendencies. (And they wonder why men are fleeing the church like sailors on a sinking ship.)

I'm not saying that we dads don't need some correction or even a good kick in the butt at times. But on Father's Day? Really?

This is supposed to be a day to honor what we have done, not blast all the ways we haven't done it.

Whether it's fathering or managing, loving or leading, serving or sacrificing, the battle is always fiercest around the places where we have not been batting a thousand. And the critics are endless. The church, our friends, spouses, even Oprah and Jerry Springer, feed into our deep awareness of our personal weaknesses. The odds can seem overwhelming, a thousand to one. Everyone is against us, and just 'cause we're paranoid doesn't mean that they're *not* out to get us!

Here's the key to winning these vast battles: don't waste your time fighting the infantry; rather, direct your forces at the commander of their army. You see, "Our struggle is not against flesh and blood, but against the rulers, against the authorities, against the powers of this dark world and against the spiritual forces of evil in the heavenly realms" (Ephesians 6:12). It is to Satan himself that we must take the fight.

Picking Your Fights

We walk away from our spouses, blow up at the kids, quit going to church, and secretly sabotage our workplaces. But those things are the "flesh and the blood" that Paul refers to in the Ephesians passage. They are not our enemy, and they are not the areas where we are to direct our fight. "For though we live in the world, we do not wage war as the world does. The weapons we fight with are not the weapons of the world" (2 Corinthians 10:3–4).

THE HEROIC PATH

Of course, it's easier to take our fights to people we can see. They are the ones who get in our faces. They're the ones who incite bad emotions in us in the first place. They deserve what they get in return. They could show some restraint and keep their mouths shut. What kind of men would we be if we just let it go, let them walk all over us?

That's not what I am suggesting. I'm not proposing that we become whimpering Christians, avoiding confrontation and becoming passive-aggressive punching bags while developing ticking time bombs in our souls. As men, we sometimes need to confront and correct. But we go wrong when we identify the other guy (or gal) as the enemy and seek to take him out or at least give him a good licking.

No, our struggle is not against people who offend us, but against something darker, deeper, and much more dangerous. That is what needs to become our target—at which we learn to direct our God-given aggression.

If ever there was a man who understood and fought this fight well, it was John the Baptist. Jesus, in speaking of him, said, "Among those born of women there has not risen anyone greater than John the Baptist; yet he who is least in the kingdom of heaven is greater than he. From the days of John the Baptist until now, the kingdom of heaven has been forcefully advancing, and forceful men lay hold of it" (Matthew 11:11–12). John was never afraid to back down from confrontation. But he also understood that the kingdom of heaven is opposed, requiring a supernatural force to advance it, and that it was the work of forceful men (read that, *warriors*) to lay hold of it.

Body Armor

Our job is to figure out how to advance God's kingdom. How do we fight these battles? In answer, let's take a look at the resources we have available to us. Paul names them for us in Ephesians, chapter six:

> Therefore put on the full armor of God, so that when the day of evil comes, you may be able to stand your ground, and after you have done everything, to stand. Stand firm then, with the belt of truth buckled around your waist, with the breastplate of righteousness in place, and with your feet fitted with the readiness that comes from the gospel of peace. In addition to all this, take up the shield of faith, with which you can extinguish all the flaming arrows of the evil one. Take the helmet of salvation and the sword of the Spirit, which is the word of God. And pray in the Spirit on all occasions with all kinds of prayers and requests. With this in mind, be alert and always keep on praying for all the saints. (Ephesians 6: 13–18)

I was doing a radio interview about my first book, *The Unseen War*, when the talk show host made an interesting comment. She stated that she has tried, repeatedly, to "put on the armor of God" each day before she goes to work, but that it didn't ever seem to work. Despite going over every part, she still felt shot down and wounded by the end of the day.

I believe my host's error lay in viewing God's armor as something similar to her wardrobe which she examines every morning before deciding what to wear to work. But that's not what Paul has in mind. He isn't thinking of something that we take off in the evening prior to a good night's sleep, then put back on again piece by piece the following morning. Paul simply tells us to put on the armor of God, so that when the day of trouble comes—and we have no idea when or where that may be—we will be ready. Our weapons are not just items that we store in our footlocker while we wait for the battle cry to sound. Rather, they are a lifestyle of changing who we are.

Keep Your Pants On

Take the first article in Paul's list, the belt of truth. The imagery here is dramatic. For a warrior, the belt is the glue that holds the rest of the uniform together. It keeps your pants up and your shirt tucked in, provides something to hang your sword on, and gives you freedom to move without getting tangled up in the rest of your weaponry.

The problem is that your belt, the thing that holds everything else together, is truth. You can't just get up one day and decide to "put on truth." Truth is something that you know (or don't know) in the deepest part of your knowing. It is something you learn to trust as absolute.

For modern-day warriors, truth may be a matter of knowing that your loved ones are in harm's way unless you act, or that the evil you are fighting must be extinguished. It may be faith in your weapon and your ability to use it. Likewise, truth involves trust in your backup—your comrades and your Commander.

Truth includes knowing the landscape of the battlefield, understanding your role in the offensive, and reckoning honestly with your own weaknesses and your enemy's strengths.

This kind of truth takes months and even years of study and experience. You don't just jump in the chopper and shoot through narrow mountain passes without spending many hours studying and knowing your bird.

This is where reading the Scriptures regularly comes in. But it's important to do so with the right motive. It's not about looking good or impressing your family and friends with your daily, in-depth study habit. Never make yourself the measure of how serious others are about pursuing God; just focus on searching for truth about your life, your family, your God, and your circumstances.

Assuming the right attitude, you *should* be reading the Bible every day, or at least regularly. It is impossible to put on the belt of truth apart from steeping yourself in the Scriptures. You can "claim" the belt of truth all day long to no effect; you have to *know* the truth, inside and out. That's why you need to study the Scriptures. It's why you need to set aside time in order to be alone with God: so you can learn truth.

Satan is called a deceiver and the Father of Lies. Everything he constructs in this world is designed to undermine truth, and simply living in this war zone bombards you with his lies. Countering them daily with truth is your only defense. Without the belt of truth, the rest of the armor just falls to the ground.

THE HEROIC PATH

Preventing Premature Heart Failure

As with the belt of truth, merely stating that we're putting on the breastplate of righteousness without understanding what it is amounts to little more than a magical mantra. But as we come to understand the righteousness of Christ and the cost He paid to transfer it to us as a guard for our hearts, it becomes the power of God Himself, covering our most vital of organs.

Jesus was not murdered at the mere whim of some crazy, mixed-up crowd. Our Lord made this clear in John 10:18 when He said, "No one takes [my life] from me, but I lay it down of my own accord." Again, later before Pilate He explained, "You would have no power over me if it were not given to you from above" (John 19:11). Jesus laid down His life, it wasn't taken from Him. He purposely submitted to death for us. For *you*. Why? So that He could "become for us wisdom from God—that is, *our righteousness*, holiness and redemption." (1 Corinthians 1:30, emphasis mine).

That's why Paul can tell us that we are "to put off your old self, which is being corrupted by its deceitful desires; to be made new in the attitude of your minds; and to put on the new self, created to be like God in true righteousness and holiness" (Ephesians 4:22–24). Paul says these things because righteousness is our new identity! Who we were, what we've done—these things no longer define who we are!

Jesus, by His own power and will, gave us something that only He had: righteousness. Rightness of heart. We don't put it on by trying to be holy or by acting religious. It is an inheritance that has been entrusted to us through the death and resurrection of our Lord Jesus, and it comes to us by way of exchange: His life for ours, His holiness for our ungodliness.

The way that we "put on the new self" is through faith. Not faith generated in our mind, convincing us that something is true, but rather, faith that comes from walking with Jesus, experiencing His righteousness in our lives; feeling the pain and failure of walking away from that righteousness and longing to have it cover us once again; and subsequently discovering the confidence that emerges when we realize that Christ's righteousness never left us in the first place. It is that kind of righteousness that covers our hearts like a breastplate.

Ready, Set ...

What does it mean to outfit your feet "with the readiness that comes from the gospel of peace"? This part of our preparation is an act of the will. A warrior's duty is to be ready for action at a moment's notice.

You don't have to do this. You can sleep in, you can choose to take a weekend off—or a lifetime. But you cannot reclaim your life unless you are ready to move, and move now. That is the reality of battle and of an enemy. Especially, your Enemy. He has time on his side and he is infinitely patient.

If your idea of fighting is to engage only on your terms, when you are ready and in a place of your choosing, well ... you'll probably win most of your skirmishes because your opponent won't even be there. He'll be waiting patiently until you're sitting with your comrades around the campfire, at ease, overfed, over-drunk, telling stories of your heroics. That's when your enemy will ambush you and the real fighting will begin: not in your timing, but in Satan's.

Think about it. Aren't the times when you've been least prepared also the times when you've been wounded the worst, taken out, pronounced incompetent for the task?

Your feet must always be battle-ready, because Satan strikes at the most inopportune moments ...

You've just had an ugly fight with your wife, you're alone at a bar, and suddenly a drink appears in front of you, courtesy of that pretty girl in the booth over there.

Your boss has been a jerk, insensitive to the incredible economic pressures you and your family face—and now an accounting error invites you to transfer company funds to your bank account.

A friend has hurt you for the final time, and you're tempted to put him out of your life for good—not out of defense or protection, but just out of spite.

These are the times when the battle is at your fire pit and your feet had better be ready. Staying alert will require a daily and even minute-by-minute decision to keep your boots laced, because you never know when the alarm will sound.

The good news is, Jesus has sent His Spirit to walk with you, sustaining and encouraging you and helping you to remain ever-vigilant. And although you must choose to be ready, you also have available One who will walk that long road with you, sustaining and encouraging when no one else will. The time to work on your relationship with the Spirit is now, not in the heat of the battle. You've heard that advice all of your Christian life, I'm sure: "Spend time with Jesus. Let His Spirit love on you." Perhaps that wisdom never seemed very relevant. But it *is* relevant. When the firefight begins, you need the confidence that comes from knowing the One who stands with you and hearing Him clearly.

Shields Up!

Few pieces of armor are counterfeited more than the shield of faith. Much of what passes for faith today reminds me of a pair of cheap sunglasses that someone slapped an Oakley sticker on. I hear it all the time: "Well, I'm just believin' Jesus for my deliverance." (Add your favorite televangelist accent as needed.) Most of the time it isn't true. Most of the time, what we're really saying is that we don't know what to do, or we simply don't want to act on what we do know, and either way we are hoping that Jesus will deliver us.

And that's okay. It's okay to hope that Jesus will deliver us. It's just not the shield of faith that Paul talks about.

Hebrews 11:1 tells us that "faith is being sure of what we hope for and certain of what we do not see." *Sure* of what we hope for? *Certain* of what we do not see? How do we get there?

The answer lies in the forging process.

Shields, at least metal shields, are forged. Forging is the process of shaping and compressing metal to produce a stronger end product. Jesus's brother James explains the faith-forging process: "Consider it pure joy, my brothers, whenever you face trials of many kinds, because you know that the testing of your faith develops perseverance. Perseverance must finish its work so that you may be mature and complete, not lacking anything" (James 1:2–4).

Bottom line: Life forges your shield of faith. The process can't be shortcut and it can't be rushed. You can't just decide to have faith. You can choose to trust and you should choose to trust, for that will help in developing faith. But faith itself comes from a lifetime of choosing to trust and of enduring some pretty dark stuff along the way.

So try this next time you find yourself in the midst of a real mess: decide to trust Jesus through whatever you face—not to make your life easier or to cover up your lack of effort or ability, but rather as an opportunity to forge the shield of faith so it becomes stronger. I predict you will find that it becomes increasingly effective at extinguishing the "flaming arrows of the evil one."

Brain Bucket

The helmet of salvation is the next piece of God's armor with which we are to ready ourselves.

By the way, exactly what are we readying ourselves for? It would be good to know; otherwise everything we're talking about is purely academic.

Paul says we're outfitting ourselves "so that when the day of evil comes, you may be able to stand your ground" (Ephesians 6:13). Notice that Paul uses the word *when*, not *if*. The day of evil will come—count on it. Most likely it has come into your life already in some way at some time. And it will come again. Maybe today, maybe tomorrow, but it will come. The day of evil is dynamic, never static. That's why we prepare for it now.

The helmet of salvation is likewise dynamic. It moves with us. Every time we turn our head, it turns too. When we stand up, its protection remains secure. And when we finally lie in our graves, it will still be accompanying us.

Our salvation, which is the finished work of Christ, reaches from our past to our present and into our future. Let's unpack all three aspects of that truth. First, Jesus *has* saved us from our sins. All that stuff of our past is taken care of. Satan, the "Accuser of the brethren," may try to use our past sins against us, but as we recall the work of Christ, the Devil's arrows of accusation fail to penetrate.

The helmet of salvation also *will* save us. When all the battles cease, in the end, we win. We have eternity with Jesus promised to us. What does that mean for us here and now? It means no worries. The worst that can happen is, we die and spend eternity in our new home.

So we've been saved and we will be saved. What we often forget, however, is that our salvation is also saving us right now, day by day. All that the world, the Enemy, and our own flesh throws at us; all of the times when we fall and sin; everything is covered in the blood of Jesus. No longer do we need to run to the temple and offer yet another sin offering. No longer must we leave the presence of God to observe a period of ritual uncleanness. All the requirements of the Law have been met for us in the salvation of Jesus Christ.

THE HEROIC PATH

Do you know what that means? It means you can quit punishing yourself. It means you can totally mess up, and yet as soon as you recognize your failure and repent, it's over. Back into the battle, baby! That's what your helmet does for you: it saves you from deadly head wounds.

Study and learn about the salvation of Jesus Christ, all He has accomplished for you. Read the book of Ephesians thoroughly and pay special attention to every appearance of the phrase "in Christ." Paul uses it over and over as he reminds us who we really are.

One thing I have found about helmets—whether they're motorcycle helmets, rock climbing helmets, football helmets, or what have you—is that I am always bolder when I wear one. I am willing to take more risks. Understanding your helmet of salvation will do the same for you.

The Pointy Thing

The crowning glory of any soldier is his weapon. It is what makes him dangerous, a force to be reckoned with. And what a weapon we possess! "Sharper than any double-edged sword," the writer of Hebrews says of it; "living and active … it penetrates even to dividing soul and spirit, joints and marrow" (Hebrews 4:12). This is no Sunday school boy's plastic toy. It is the identical weapon that the Son of God used to defeat the Enemy: the Word of God. You'll do well to know it, and know it well.

There is a great scene in the movie *The Mask of Zorro* when Alejandro, the young Zorro, is beginning his training as a swordsman. The master, Don Diego de la Vega, asks Alejandro if he knows how to use his sword. "Of course!" he replies. "The pointy end goes into the other man."

Yes, that's true: sticking the pointy end of a sword into an opponent can cause him a lot of harm. However, if that is all we know how to do with our weapon, then we will fall far short of utilizing its full capabilities. And as de la Vega warned Alejandro, we will likely fight bravely but die quickly. The real power comes through proper training.

Ask any professional athlete, Army marksman, or even a great cook how he got to be so good. None of them will tell you that they were born that way. They trained, every one of them. We tend to miss this in our media-flooded culture. Watching a NASCAR driver effortlessly maneuvering or an NBA star floating up for a slam dunk, we rarely stop to consider the years of training required to attain such expertise.

Our spiritual lives are similar. Reading about the Billy Grahams and Martin Luthers of the faith, we incorrectly assume that they just decided one day to take God's Word and go to work. What we don't see are the years of training and listening to God that got such people to where their lives have shaped countless other lives.

While we are on that subject, let me also say that I believe the Word of God is more than just the written word (although I do believe that is the final say in any disagreement of what God is saying). The Bible identifies Jesus himself as the Word, and as such, we have relationship and communication with Him. Don't miss that part of your weapon against our enemy. Learn to hear His voice, to heed his warnings.

Finally, Pray

Prayer is the last piece of armor listed in the Ephesians passage, but it is by no means the least. Chapter six, verse 18, tells us to pray "on all occasions with all kinds of prayers and requests." Notice the alls. All occasions. All kinds of prayers. All kinds of requests. Nothing is off limits here. Everything should be included. No concern is too small or too big or too stupid or too arrogant. Let God sort all of that out. You pray. Don't even think about going onto the battlefield without praying.

Entire books have been written on prayer. I'll leave it to you to find one you like. But honestly, the simplest approach is to just pray. God will work out the details.

TRAIL MARKERS

1. Often we fight the wrong enemy. "We walk away from our spouses, blow up at the kids, quit going to church, and secretly sabotage our workplaces." Where have you been bringing your fights to? Why?
2. Describe the process of "putting on the belt of truth."
3. What is the breastplate of righteousness?
4. What are the times when your spiritual feet are the least ready to move?
5. What opportunities do you have currently to forge your shield of faith? Are you willing to embrace them as opportunities?
6. Name the three parts of salvation discussed in the text.
7. What activities are you engaged in that can help you know and use your sword better? What activities are you willing to engage in?

Chapter Eighteen

Aboriginal Living Skills

Disappointment to a noble soul is what cold water is to burning metal; it strengthens, tempers, intensifies, but never destroys it.

Eliza Tabor, American Author

In this world you will have trouble.

Jesus, Author of Life

John 16:33

THE HEROIC PATH

I've always wanted to take a wilderness survival course. I'm not talking about one of those reality TV shows where they leave you on a deserted island "alone" for a one-hour episode with twenty other contestants, a full television crew, makeup artists, and a hospitality tent. No, I'm thinking something more like the Aboriginal Living Skills School (ALSS) in Arizona.

At ALSS, an experienced backwoods survivalist takes you out in the desert and instructs you on the skills necessary to make your own shelter as well as your own tools and weapons. You then have to use your training to find your own food while dealing with the multiple curve balls that nature throws at you. No cell phones, no computers, no air conditioning or camper trailers or microwaves or water faucets. Just bare-bones survival like our ancestors experienced for thousands of years.

My problem is, I just don't have enough motivation to fork out the twenty-five hundred bucks it costs to take the course, not to mention the two-week time commitment. Sure, it would be cool, but what are the chances that I would ever use what I learned? I'm really not much of a doomsday worrier, so my incentive for such an investment is minimal. I just cannot imagine a world without Wal-Mart, my pickup truck, and refrigeration. Still ... it sure would be fun, wouldn't it?

This same mindset has permeated our western culture Christianity. Even if we do believe that the Devil is real and that our life in Christ is opposed, still we doubt that we will ever face any real danger. We can always depend on grace (the Wal-Mart of our faith, supplying everything we need), our local church body

Aboriginal Living Skills

to carry us along when we're exhausted (our trusty pickup), and Jesus's promise to always be with us (a faith preservative better than any refrigerator).

Yet, while all of these things are true, Jesus didn't ask us to merely hang on until the end. He invited us to *live* life—His life. He died so that we could advance God's kingdom, live out our place in His story, and bear much fruit. And this manner of living teeters constantly on the precipice of a wilderness experience.

How, then, do we prepare to survive that wilderness—and not just survive, but flourish? How do we become spiritual Navy Seals, developing the aboriginal living skills necessary to survive the myriad natural and supernatural disasters that await our life in Christ?

The sad truth is that many of us don't cultivate such skills. Oh, we put out an effort occasionally. We attend a conference or two, maybe sign up for Sunday school. We buy books like this one with the best of intentions. Sermons move us, prayer hones us, Scripture enlightens us, and fellow warriors sharpen us. But still we feel so ill-prepared. Like Dorothy in *The Wizard of Oz*, we find ourselves suddenly in a strange land with strange creatures all around and evil hunting us.

All we want is to get back to Kansas.

I've done my best to outline the battle that has been set against your heart; to help you find healing for your heart and your place in God's epic story; and to offer some instruction on preparing for the battles that are yet to come. This book is just a primer, I know, but it's a start. However, as every wilderness survival expert will tell you, you can only learn so much in the classroom. Eventually you need to get out into the wilds and begin to use and refine what you've been taught.

But how will I survive? Will I survive? What will happen when I walk out the back door into this adventure with Christ, and the bullets start flying?

Where Am I and What Just Happened?

Any Boy Scout can tell you that the first thing to do when disaster strikes is to Stop. Take a deep breath. Get a hold of yourself. And then, amid the chaos, reorient to the situation.

Too often we do just the opposite: we panic. That's what happened a number of years ago at a motocross event I was attending. A boy in his teens was working on a large, hundred-foot tabletop jump. He had somehow managed to enlist his mom to stand next to the obstacle and photograph him as he displayed some very cool mid-air moves. But one of his tricks didn't go quite as planned, and the young man hit the ground pretty hard.

Mom, instead of surveying the scene, instinctively ran out to check on her boy. That's when a second rider hit the long runway of the giant tabletop. Not until he was in the air could see the mom on the backside of the jump. He hit her in the chest while he was still airborne.

The rider was okay, the son had a broken leg, but the woman suffered a punctured lung, numerous broken bones, and a concussion.

Our first key to survival, then, is not to react but to reorient. Especially when all hell is breaking out, it's wise to ask, "Where am I and what just happened?" This simple question can produce such insight that when we finally slow down enough to consider it, we're often embarrassed that we didn't do so sooner.

I had such an experience earlier this week. My wife was heading home Sunday evening after taking my younger son to her parents' home in Nebraska. She called me at 5:00 p.m. stating that she was sitting on the side of the road with smoke rolling out of her engine. The transmission on her 200,000-mile minivan had overheated. I drove the sixty miles to pick her up and dropped the van off at our mechanic's garage.

The next day my older son called to report that he could not meet me for our usual workout because he had blown a tire on his car. Since our other son was out of town, I suggested that he drive his brother's car to the gym. Upon arriving, he commented on how well his brother's brakes worked—thus revealing that his own brakes required serious repairs.

The following day, my wife, driving our younger son's car, suddenly lost the power steering in the only dependable transportation we had left.

That was about the last straw. Disoriented, shell-shocked, and wondering where I was going to come up with the finances to fix all of these vehicles at the same time, I panicked. With my day turned to toast, I became short-tempered and frustrated. But then, by the grace of God, I remembered to ask the question, "Where am I and what just happened? What is really going on here?"

That's when I remembered the Scripture verse I had read earlier that morning:

"My son, do not make light of the Lord's discipline, and do not lose heart when he rebukes you, because the Lord disciplines those he loves" (Hebrews 12:5–6). Was this my Father's discipline? Maybe it was just bad luck. It could even be a direct attack from Satan. It didn't matter. If it was discipline, Jesus was doing it because He loved me. If it was bad luck, well, hey, it's all His anyway. And if the Devil was behind it, it wasn't going to work because I knew that I was a beloved son of the King. I was not going to lose heart over a piece of metal.

"Where am I and what just happened?" is like your spiritual GPS. It gathers information from the satellites surrounding you (which, by the way, sometimes takes a few minutes), triangulates your coordinates, and then identifies your position. It doesn't change your situation, but it does tell you which side of the mountain you're on.

Three Essentials

Once you're properly oriented, your next priority is the three essentials: food, water, and shelter. Before you make further plans, these must be procured. Once you've got them, you will have the strength and safety needed for your next move. Without them, life cannot continue.

Lack of these necessities has been the Achilles heel of more than a few poor souls who have found themselves lost in the wilderness or caught on a mountain by a spring snowstorm. Desperate, they attempted to find their way out, powered by the adrenalin pulsing through their veins. But hours turned into days, the weather worsened, and the fear that had fueled them earlier could no longer override the progressive glycogen deficit that was building in their overworked, underfed, muscles. Ultimately they succumbed to exposure, dehydration, and starvation.

The saddest thing is that often when their bodies were found, shelter, food, or water was just moments away. The victims simply hadn't looked.

Isn't it interesting that Jesus variously refers to Himself as each of the three survival essentials:

Shelter
"O Jerusalem, Jerusalem, you who kill the prophets and stone those sent to you, how often I have longed to gather your children together, as a hen gathers her chicks under her wings, but you were not willing!" (Luke 13:34).

Food
"I am the bread of life. He who comes to me will never go hungry " (John 6:35).

Water
Jesus answered her, "If you knew the gift of God and who it is that asks you for a drink, you would have asked him and he would have given you living water" (John 4:10).

THE HEROIC PATH

It's no coincidence, you know, that Jesus offers Himself as our shelter, sustenance, and life-giving water. In John 16:33, He told His disciples, "In this world you will have trouble." He knew it was going to be hard. He knew He was inviting us on a dangerous mission. He knew we would find times of disorientation and absolute hopelessness. So He did not sugar-coat the situation; rather, Jesus was straight-up with His followers: "You *will* have trouble" (emphasis mine).

But do you remember the rest of Jesus's statement? In the same breath, without hesitating, Jesus finishes the thought: "But take heart! I have overcome the world."

Our King's answer to the question, Why do bad things happen to good people? provides more than an explanation (i.e. this world is a dangerous place). It also helps us survive tough times by pointing us to Jesus Himself as our food, refreshment, and protection.

Some years ago, singer-songwriter Natalie Grant released an incredible, gut wrenchingly honest song that she titled *Held*. In it she tells the story of a mother losing her child despite months of godly, Spirit-led prayers. Grant goes on to pen the nagging question that so many have faced: that to think of such a loss as Providence, at least on this side of eternity, is appalling. Yet, she reasons, "Why should we be saved from nightmares?" And that question leads to one of the most profound choruses I have ever heard:

This is what it means to be held,

how it feels when the sacred is torn from your life and

you survive.

> This is what it is to be loved and to know
> that the promise was that when everything fell, we'd be held.[9]

That's life support. That is your food, water, and shelter. In the midst of the storm, before reacting and running and panicking, as soon as you gather your bearings, find Jesus. He is the only One who can sustain you so that you can fight another day. Without Him, your energy and passion will soon wane, and like so many others, you too will become another unnecessary casualty of the storm.

Experience: The Ultimate Training Ground

You've reoriented yourself to your circumstances. You're in tune with Jesus as your life support. Now it's time to evaluate what exactly it was that got you where you are in the first place.

I once read that it takes most of a lifetime to become a truly great mountaineer. The reason isn't conditioning or stamina or technical ability; most teenagers can develop those. The reason is experience. In extreme mountaineering, whether on Everest or Denali or Patagonia, the greatest risk is not running out of energy or oxygen, or slipping on a technical section; the biggest opposition to your success is the mountain itself, with the myriad conditions it can throw at you: Blinding snow. Howling winds. Avalanches. Crevasses, rockfall, and the like. Only veterans of mountain conditions, who have repeatedly survived every conceivable kind of

---

9 "Held," copyright 2005 by Natalie Grant.

THE HEROIC PATH

natural disaster as well as their own mistakes, and who have learned from them all, know how to handle all the manifold challenges of the peaks.

Our charge as Christians is not to avoid making mistakes. Rather, it is to learn from our mistakes and grow. The learning opportunities will come—because you will encounter disaster on your journey with your King. Count on it. You'll get off course. Satan's arrows will pierce your armor. Your sword will become dull and your faith will be shaken. But such experiences have served to train the greatest heroes of faith, and they will train you as well.

So, again, let's look at what got you here and how you have been responding to your situation. Serious introspection and honesty are required. The point of this frank self-assessment is not to condemn you or parade your failures before you. It's to train you, much as a coach might show a video of a botched play to help his players understand what they should have done differently.

Satan, your enemy, will undoubtedly be in the viewing room with you, and he will try to demoralize you:

"Look how you failed again."

"That was pitiful."

"You'll never get this."

Simply recognize such thoughts as the voice of the Accuser and dismiss them. Satan is a liar and lying is all he can do. Using small bits of truth, he twists them into apparent absolutes. In response, you'll find it helpful to actually speak out loud to Satan: "What you say is not true. I am a child of the King, a co-heir with

Jesus, and I claim His righteousness as mine. I cover my failures with the blood of Jesus, and by the authority He has given me, I command you to flee right now—you and all of your foul and unclean spirits and thoughts." Then ask Jesus to feed and nourish you by His Spirit.

During my initial training as a physician, I was told that I would need to become a lifelong learner, always adapting and adjusting to the changing world of medicine. We as Christians likewise need to be lifelong learners, adapting to the different attacks of our enemy and adjusting our tactics. Crises will come; the question is, will we learn from them?

Adaptation

Adaptation: that is the final step to survival. While it is good to learn from our mistakes, apprehension without application is useless. We need to act on what we have learned, change something about how we proceed.

You've heard it said that the definition of insanity is doing the same thing over and over again while expecting different results. By that definition, I fear that much of my walk with Christ has been insanity, and I suspect you could say the same. We find ourselves in a familiar sin or setback, we vow never to repeat it, we recommit ourselves to Jesus, and yet somehow we end up right back in the same mess that started the whole thing. The problem is that we never really changed anything. We didn't seek counseling or study what the Scriptures have to say on the matter. We didn't

THE HEROIC PATH

find comrades to walk with us and fortify our armor. Or if we did do these things, we either let them slide or else we did them the same say as before, which obviously didn't work.

The other side of this coin is that our enemy changes his tactics; so yes, you may have done everything right and he may have just found another chink in your armor. If that is the case, then you know the area in your life where you need to adapt. The point is, the crises in our lives create opportunities to learn, change, and walk more closely with Jesus.

Of course, they also offer great excuses to just give up. So which will you choose: reorientation, food, water, shelter, evaluation, and adjustment; or panic, confusion, and blind wandering? "In this world you will have trouble." Disaster will strike. Avalanches will happen. The only thing that is certain is uncertainty. We live in a world at war, and war is always unpredictable and filled with chaos.

But when the chaos strikes, you have an opportunity to mature in spirit, wisdom, and character. The choice is yours: wilderness survival training or another rerun of last year's reality TV.

TRAIL MARKERS

1. When have you found yourself thrust into a situation in which you needed to know where you were and what just happened?
2. When the life's storms hit, where do you normally run for food, water, and shelter?
3. Look back at a recent crisis in your life. What can you learn from it about yourself, your enemy, and God?
4. What can you do differently to handle a future disaster with a better-honed, survival-skill mentality?

Chapter Nineteen

Off with the Fig Leaf

*The greatest glory in living lies not in never falling,
but in rising every time we fall.*

Nelson Mandela

*He who began a good work in you will carry it
on to completion until the day of Christ Jesus.*

Philippians 1:6

THE HEROIC PATH

Mike was twenty-three years old and living his dream. Fresh out of flight school and already making a living as a charter pilot, he could think of nothing else that he would rather do. Since his boyhood he had dreamt of flying, idolized pilots, and studied airplanes with the intensity of a brain surgeon. Mike lived and breathed aeronautics.

As a young pilot, Mike was eager to prove his worth and was willing to work hard to do so. When asked if he would take a couple of businessmen on a routine trip, Mike jumped at the opportunity. He would be flying a Cessna Turbo 210, a small single-engine, high-performance, general aviation aircraft. Although Mike had never flown this particular aircraft before, he had logged hundreds of hours in similar planes. After quickly reviewing the procedures unique to this aircraft and topping off the fuel, he took off with his passengers.

The flight was smooth and uneventful—that is, until a few miles from their destination, when suddenly the airplane's only engine quit. Mike was able to get it restarted, but only for a minute. It died again, and this time there was no restarting it. It seems that this particular plane had a unique method that was supposed to be followed during the fueling process. Mike had neglected to recognize this, and now he was out of fuel.

There was no hope of making it to the airport. Quickly assessing his options, the young pilot chose to set his plane down at the only place he could find: a neighborhood street. Considering the circumstances, it was a skillful landing. The plane clipped a tree and flipped upside down, yet all of its occupants remained conscious as the plane came to a rest in a driveway.

It wasn't until hours later, while Mike was being evaluated at the local hospital, that he got the tragic news. One of his passengers, a man who had refused initial medical care after assisting the others out of the wreckage, had died of internal injuries.

Suddenly Mike's dream had become a nightmare. A man who had trusted him was dead, the man's family devastated, and Mike's career likely over.

Scott was a successful entrepreneur. He was running three separate ventures, had just built his dream home, was married to a godly woman, and had been blessed with three sons. He was actively involved in his church discipling other men and would regularly bring up his success and the trappings of wealth, firmly believing that his identity could never rest on what he had accomplished, but only on Christ alone. Those convictions were about to be refined in the fire.

One of Scott's businesses was in the area of an investment partnership. In the volatile markets that marked the first decade of the twenty-first century, investments were hard to read, and despite extensive research and planning, this one was not panning out. Scott had lost about sixty percent of his partners' initial investments, a total of about 1.6 million dollars.

Then someone raised the question of fraud. The Securities and Exchange Commission (SEC) got involved and an investigation ensued. All of Scott's assets were frozen, meaning he could no longer pay creditors and employees or continue running his two other very successful businesses. Friends abandoned Scott, ministries asked him to resign, and legal fees consumed what little

THE HEROIC PATH

resources he had left. In a matter of a few months, a man who once had everything was flat broke, living in his parents' basement, writhing in the pain of what had become a public attack on his character. The investigation failed to find Scott guilty of any wrongdoing, but it was too little too late.

That's when the other shoe fell. Disregarding the fact that the SEC had cleared Scott, the State Securities Commissioner chose to bring charges. Penniless, Scott was forced to fight his case with a $400 budget using a public defender. Having defended mostly rape, murder, and burglary cases, Scott's attorney had no understanding at all of investment laws.

After months of fighting and stalling, the ordeal was taking a real toll on Scott's wife, his children, and his own health. With no other options available, Scott pled *nolo contendere* ("I will not contest"). He was ordered to pay the 1.6 million dollars back and was sentenced to fifteen months in the state prison system.

It is possible—no, it is probable—that your life has likewise not followed the script you had expected. Maybe you didn't end up in prison or with a dead man on your conscience. Or maybe you have. In any case, there have almost certainly been times when, like Mike and Scott, you have failed miserably and felt the bitter lash of exposure. During those times, not only have you suffered, but so have others whom your life has touched. Family, friends, adversaries, even total strangers—all have in some way experienced the ripple effect of your failure.

Yet, painful as it is, such circumstances can become the turning point of your life.

Regaining Your Glory

Most of us grow up with a significant shot of narcissism pulsing through our veins. As young men, we really do believe that the world is at our fingertips and that there is something special about us. Anything is possible, even likely, at least within the realm of our giftings. This sense of uniqueness and optimism is the beauty of youth, and it is also part of the anointing of our God. He was the One who told us to "Be fruitful and increase in number; fill the earth and subdue it. Rule over the fish of the sea and the birds of the air and over every living creature that moves on the ground" (Genesis 1:28).

The difficulty, as we've already established, is that life doesn't usually turn out that way. The Serpent shows up, we succumb to his propaganda, eat the apple, and suddenly are left scrambling, looking for a fig leaf to cover our previous glory, which has now become our shame. John Eldredge writes in *Wild at Heart* that "most of what you encounter when you meet a man is a facade, an elaborate fig leaf, a brilliant disguise."[10]

The dilemma then becomes: how do you lose the fig leaf and step back into the glory of your life? You can only sit in the classroom for so long. Introspection and self-assessment are healthy activities to a point. After a while, though, they become a pathological obsession. Healing is good and beautiful if it actually brings healing and restoration; but if the only purpose of repentance is to demonstrate your humility, then it really isn't

---

10 John Eldredge, *Wild at Heart: Discovering the Secret of a Man's Soul* (Nashville: Thomas Nelson, 2001), 52.

repentance, is it? No wonder the "healing" doesn't stick. And what's the purpose of training and learning if there is no place to use the skills they instill? Armchair quarterbacks might be fine on Super Bowl Sunday, but come Monday morning, they don't own a championship ring.

What we need is a plan. We need a diagram, the simpler the better, of how to step back into the story that is our lives. And as luck would have it, we have just such an illustration in the last chapter of John's gospel.

The scene is set during the forty days after Jesus's resurrection, before He ascended into heaven. It centers around one person—a man who had known the power of walking with Jesus, had experienced some of the most miraculous events in the history of mankind, and had heard from the lips of Jesus Himself what his life's calling was: to be a fisher of men.

But he had fallen asleep, leaving Jesus to pray alone during His hour of greatest need. He had cut off a man's ear only to have his Master tell him to put his sword away. And worst of all, in the courtyard of the high priest he had bitterly denied even knowing Jesus. Those eyes of Jesus looking back at him … he would never forget those eyes.

So what did Peter do? He went back to fishing—not for men, but for fish. He knew how to do that. It wasn't that he didn't believe in Jesus any longer. He had seen Him after His resurrection, in Peter's own home, eating bread. With his own eyes he had witnessed the empty grave. He had watched Thomas put his hand in the wounds in Jesus's side. But still, Peter just couldn't shed the fig leaf. His shame was too much, his failure too great. So he went fishing.

Risking the Catch

That's where the Master showed up. Not in the temple, pacing about and waiting for Peter to pull himself back together. Rather, on the lakeshore, watching Peter struggle once again.

> Early in the morning, Jesus stood on the shore, but the disciples did not realize that it was Jesus. He called out to them, "Friends, haven't you any fish?" (John 21:4–5)

Ouch! That's gotta sting. Not only was Peter not much of a fisher of men, he apparently wasn't much of a fisher of fish either. And I love how Jesus points it out: *This is not who you are anymore, Peter.* Then comes the defining moment. "Throw your net on the right side of the boat," yells Jesus, "and you will find some."

Peter didn't even realize it was Jesus speaking yet, but he had a decision to make. He remembered another time when Someone told him to throw a net out. And surely he remembered the results. Would Peter do it again? Would he risk again?

What were the chances of the same trick being successful a second time? What was the likelihood that Peter would experience a second miraculous catch?

Peter threw out the net, and in doing so provided our first teaching point: your fig leaf may be expertly constructed, and it may have everyone else fooled, but under it is still the same man who knows the voice of the King and is known by Him. You may not immediately recognize that voice for what it is. You may think it's just a stranger on the shore interfering with your business. But deep down, Jesus's voice stirs something in you. Behind the leaf, behind the façade, your soul resonates.

And so you must act. Regardless of how silly it sounds or how much it flies in the face of your field of "expertise," you absolutely must risk responding to the Voice. I can't guarantee that you'll catch a net full of fish, but I can guarantee that your fig leaf—your false self—will begin to lose its grip on your life.

Recognizing Jesus

Over the side of the boat went Peter's net, and something miraculous happened. The net filled with fish—153 to be exact! That's when John, Pete's old fishing buddy and the narrator of the story, pointed out the obvious: "It is the Lord."

Without hesitation, without considering the freshly caught fish or his partners who needed to manage the overburdened boat, Peter jumped into the water and swam to shore. To Jesus. Pretence behind, the old Petra—the Rock—was back. It wasn't about theatrics; it was about getting back to the One whom Peter knew to be true and who knew Peter to be true as well.

This is where we often hesitate. Maybe we do take a chance—step out in faith, as it were—but when blessing follows, when we are privileged to see some fruit, we dismiss it. "Must have been just a lucky coincidence," we tell ourselves. For whatever reason, we're reluctant to attribute our success to God's anointing. Maybe it's the scars of our past failures. Maybe it's a false humility. Maybe it's just the fear of allowing hope to once again surface in the quagmire of our self-pity. Whatever the reason is, it's toxic, and we can't allow it to rob us of victory just when God is turning the tables on our behalf.

Peter and his companions netted a boatful of fish. Whatever our "fish" might look like for us, they're no coincidence, and our hesitance to recognize the Lord's hand in the matter is not the voice of common sense. It is that of our enemy. In a last-ditch effort to direct us away from what God has for us, he throws all he has our way: confusion, doubt, unbelief, lethargy, and fear. Now is not the time to reason things through in response; like Peter, we must act. We must jump into the water and start swimming before someone tells us not to.

Fortunately, the way we do so usually begins on a small scale. It may just be a nudging of the Spirit to lend a hand, say a prayer, or call a friend. In your own circumstances, as you take a step, and as you see God respond—perhaps with a thank-you or an invitation to call again—continue to move forward. You are advancing the kingdom! It's so easy to dismiss the signs that it really is Jesus standing there on the shore, but don't. Please don't. Carry on. You're getting closer to the real action.

Putting the Past Behind

Once Peter had moved back toward his Lord, it was time for Jesus to prepare His disciple for the mission ahead. So Jesus asked Peter the three "do you love me" questions (John 21:15–18). In doing so, Jesus was both testing and revealing Peter's true heart, the heart behind the fig leaf. He began by asking Peter if he loved Him "more than these," likely referring to the fishing lifestyle that Peter had returned to, or perhaps even to Peter's friends. A second time Jesus asked whether Peter loved Him unconditionally, forsaking all else: *agape* love. Finally, Jesus asked Peter if he loved Him as a brother and as a friend: *phileo* love.

A friend of mine once pointed out that when Jesus asks a question, it's not because He doesn't know the answer; it's because *we* don't (or at least, we don't think we do). Jesus knew Peter's heart. He knew that Peter loved Him more than life itself. But Jesus wanted Peter to know this as well. He wanted Peter to remember who he really was. That was Peter's only hope of stepping out of the shame of his failure and losing his fig leaf once and for all.

Jesus wants to do the same for you. One of the more confusing aspects of stepping back into the battle is the seemingly minimal support you'll receive at times. Sometimes that lack of support is the Enemy's doing, but often it is simply a test, a necessary ordeal designed to elicit a resolve in your heart that Jesus knows is there, but which you have forgotten.

For me, this book has tested that resolve. In writing about failure, my own shortcomings have pounded the shores of my heart like waves on the body-strewn beaches of Normandy. Each chapter, each sentence, has been a struggle. Doubts, distractions, apathy: all have been my constant companion. Yet somewhere deep within me, a Voice has urged me forward—not quickly, but steadily. I am in a better place today for having heeded that Voice, for it is the call of my Master. Jesus is just as interested in me walking out the glory of my life as He was in Peter walking out his—and as He is in you walking out yours.

Remember Mike, our pilot? After enduring a grueling investigation by the Federal Aviation Administration, he eventually found his way back into the captain's seat. Today Mike is a flight instructor, sharing his battle-proven wisdom with other pilots. He's also a drummer in a Christian band, keeping the rhythm of worship rocking forward, much like the rhythm of his life. There is a confidence and strength about Mike that is seldom found in a man so young.

As for Scott, after serving his time, he was released from prison and began rebuilding his life, starting with the most important part of it: his family. Having a criminal record made it harder for Scott to do business. But his giftings were obvious and his determination to make things right was powerful. In his own words, Scott was committed to being a "model of what it means to suffer in a godly manner," and consequently, God is honoring him. Scott is now the number-two man in a $22 million business. He is coaching a high school boys' swim team, and he is being the husband and father he knows he was called to be. When you talk with Scott, you can still sense bitterness and pain in his words, something he himself readily admits. But Scott is healing. He is moving forward. He is refusing to stay in the past, hiding and licking old wounds.

Mike, Scott, Peter, you, me—we are all heroes, every one of us. The heroic path is our destiny. It is what Jesus came to restore us to.

THE HEROIC PATH

We have a calling yet to fulfill, and so we are still in the battle. Someday, perhaps soon, the warfare will finally end, and on that day the pain and embarrassment of our less-than-stellar days will disappear. What will remain is what we have done with our time here: the ways in which we have risen above our pain, failures, and disappointments in order to invest in God's kingdom.

Until then, God's promise is that "he who began a good work in you will carry it on to completion until the day of Christ Jesus" (Philippians 1:6). Our part is to go, like Gideon, in the strength that we have—because our King is sending us. Jesus is sending you. He always has been.

I know that much in your life has changed. That everything has changed.

And yet, nothing has changed. You are still a son of the King.

You are still called by His name and anointed by His Spirit. You are still in the heart of the battle.

And you still have a path to follow which is yours alone. A heroic path.

TRAIL MARKERS

1. What is the greatest failure you have experienced in your life? Who were the casualties? What within you died?
2. In what ways have you, like Peter, "gone back to fishing"? What does your "fig leaf" look like these days?
3. What could you do today to risk exposure and begin dropping your fig leaf?
4. Consider your life circumstances. Where might Jesus be calling you to jump into the water and swim toward Him?
5. What are some things that test your resolve to heed Jesus's invitation? Are you willing to take up the challenge and walk with Jesus again?
6. Find a quiet place to be with your King and ask Jesus what responding to His call looks like for you. Spend some time quietly contemplating the question and listening for an answer from the Lord.

Acknowledgments

Writing a book about failure has had the effect of placing my own failings under the microscope of a very personal and painful self-condemnation. Most of us, especially men, would just as soon put those past experiences out of our thoughts, and I am certainly no different. So while I clearly felt the hand of God leading me to pen, as well as walk this heroic path, all that is opposed to our King has set itself against this journey.

As such, this project would not have been possible without so many who have traveled with me through this process.

My precious wife and the princess of my own kingdom has stood by my dreams, disappointments, depressions, distractions, apathies, and passions with the strength and poise of a heroine. Without her, I shudder to think where I may be. Thank you, Sandra.

Jim Helzer is one of those rare brothers who believes in me when no one else (including myself) does. Thank you my friend for the Starbucks mornings and for opening your heart for me. You have kept me in this battle.

As you read *The Heroic Path,* you will meet many more who have shared their own heroic paths with me, some personally, some historically, and some indirectly through the beauty of the internet. It is their stories that will give men hope for their own, and so to each of them we all owe our deepest gratitude.

Of course, dreams, stories, and even a manuscript have little effect if there is no means to present them to others. I have had the honor now of working with a number of different publishers, and I must say that none have ever compared, in terms of heart and passion for this message, like Kevin Miles and the Heart & Life team. Not only has Kevin orchestrated the best in the industry to bring together this book that makes me look much more polished than I am, but he has also become a brother and a friend. May God bless you Kev with the same honor from others that you have bestowed on me.

Finally, James the brother of Jesus wrote that we were to consider it joy when we go through trials and failures, because those are the very times when God is in the business of maturing and refining us (James 1:3-4, my paraphrase). I'm still not a big fan of the verse, but there is a deep truth in it, and as such I am eternally thankful to my heavenly Father who has fathered me through all that life has brought and all that it will bring. I love you, Dad! Keep me close as you light my own heroic path for me.

David Kortje Bio

David Kortje is a husband, father, and most importantly a son of the King of the Universe through the grace of Jesus Christ. He is also an author, speaker, and motivator whose **heart is to see the sons of God walk in all the fullness of Life that Christ has come to offer.**

David has had the honor of carrying his message of freedom in Christ through his speaking engagements, writings, and website throughout the United States, as well as Europe, Africa, Asia, and Australia. He is the director and founder of **Knight Vision Ministries.**

Giving his life to Christ in 1987 while in Medical School, David has spent the last twenty-five years in Christian ministry, leading small groups, preaching and teaching, leading retreats, and conference speaking, while also practicing medicine full time.

David received a Bachelor of Science Degree, Summa Cum Laude from the University of Nebraska Omaha, and his M.D.

from the University of Nebraska Medical Center. His experience as a physician has greatly influenced his desire to see people healed emotionally as well as spiritually.

David is the author of *The Unseen War: Winning the Fight for Life* (Parson Place Press 2009), *Your Personal Battle Plan* (AuthorHouse 2009), as well as numerous journal and newsletter articles.

Husband of twenty-eight years to Sandra, a father of four, and a very proud grandfather, David loves backpacking, rock climbing, and racing motocross in his free time.

He is available for speaking engagements. Contact him through his website: **www.knightvisionministries.com**.

Or you may email him at david@knightvisionministries.com.